Verflectin Media

SOMEHOW

Verflectin Media | San Francisco

Douglas Cruickshank

SOMEHOW
Living on Uganda Time

With an introduction to the photographs by Owen Edwards

Somehow: Living on Uganda Time

Copyright © 2013 by Douglas Cruickshank

All rights reserved. No part of this book may be used or reproduced in any manner whatsoever without written permission of the author, except in the case of brief quotations embodied in critical articles and reviews.

This book is published by Verflectin Media and was printed and bound in China.

For information about other books and to purchase photographs visit
douglascruickshank.com

Book design by Tracy Cox
coxdesignco.com

Printing coordination by Global Interprint
globalinterprint.com

First Printing: September 2013

Library of Congress Control Number: 2013939070

ISBN-13: 978-0-9893235-0-5

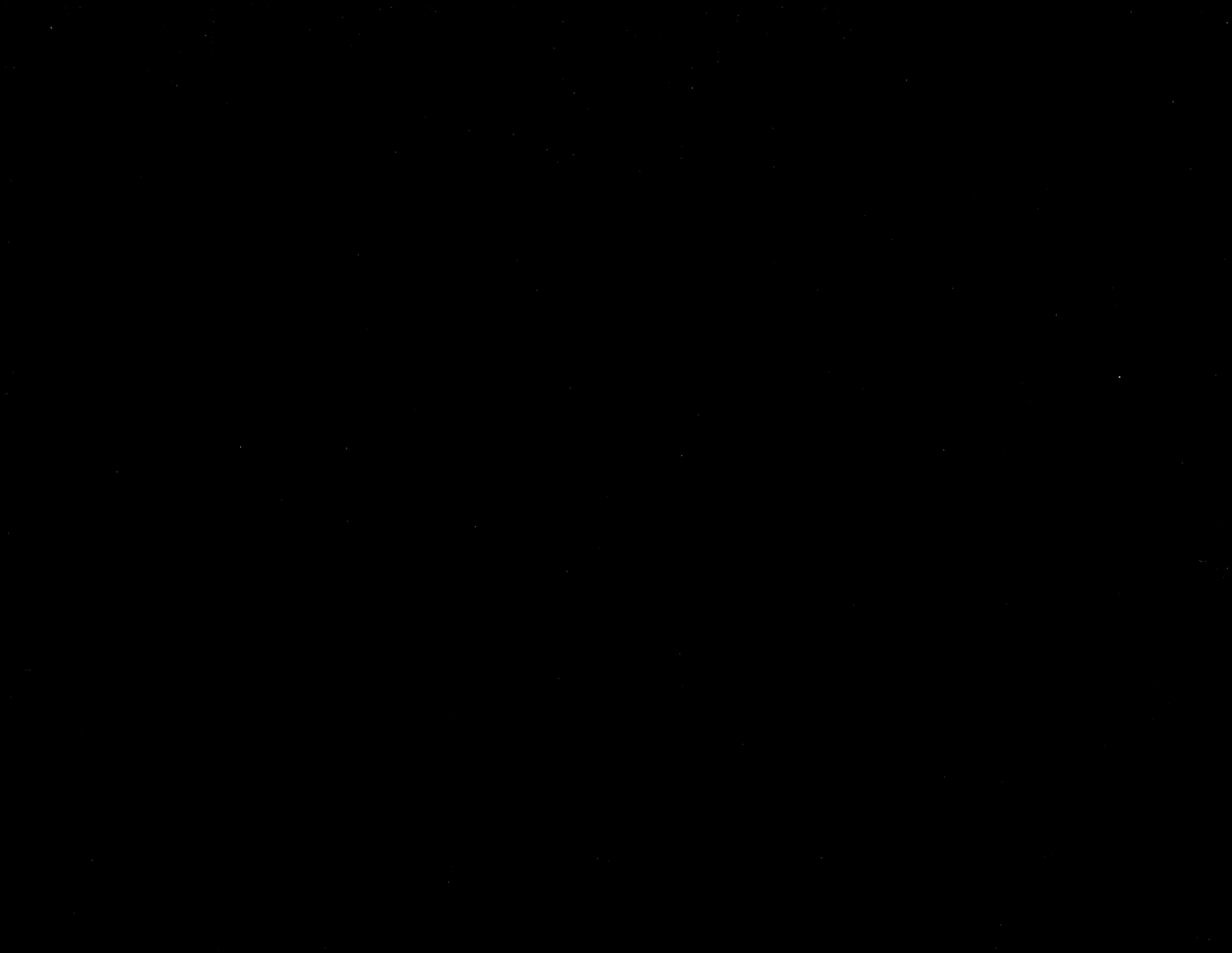

"You go away for a long time and return a different person — you never come all the way back."

—Paul Theroux

CONTENTS

Going Into Uganda Time	XXVI
A Sixth Sense *by Owen Edwards*	XXX
Omwanjakyanjakya	5
The War of the Angels in the Days of Rain	7
The Invisible Dog Choir	9
Coming into Tombstone	10
Names	11
Pterodactyls to Watch Over Us	13
African Taxi Opera	15
Vaches Sans Frontières	19
Behold the Blue-Headed Stranger	23
A Faint Recollection	25
The Devil Drives	27
What's That Sound, Elijah?	39
Bicycle of Smoke	41
Bring It	43
Spellbound on the Mountain	48
The Coherence of Coincidence	60
No One Stops the Rain	63
Slow Fade	65
You Still Workin' on That?	71

Don't It Make My Blue Mind Blown	74
Landscaping the Mountains of the Moon	77
True Fabrications	79
Drama King of the Beasts	83
Born Again	86
Department of Synchronicity	91
Attack of the Recalcitrant Mooncalves	93
Channeling	97
No Sun King	101
A Permit to Visit the Relatives	115
Chiaroscuro With Your Obundu?	117
Speaking in Tongues	118
The Well-Balanced Life	121
Invisible Africa	122
Riding With Sheena	132
Erection	137
Madeline Breaks Through	161
Archeology of a Sunlit Morning	165
Running Into an Old Friend	173
Driving a Soft Bargain	174
Crossing Kampala	177
Somehow	183

Fraternizing With the Charismatic Mega Fauna	195	Zanzibar Moon Breathing	307
Blues Dog Bites	197	Journey to No Name Island	309
Peaking	199	Scenes from a Zanzibar January	313
It's Only Rock in Road, but I Like It	203	The Sultan's Portrait	327
Heroic Toy Manufacturers of Uganda	205	In the Caves of the Shetani Cult	331
Stoptime: The Tyranny of Photography	207	The Way of the Dhow	337
Sylvia's Wedding	213	Shoes and Elephants	339
It's Only Rock in Road, II: The Burning Boulder	215	Love and Money	341
Darkness in Daytime	221	Pigmalion	351
The Lost	222	The Sensuous Rhino	353
Enos Crosses Over	225	The Apartheid Museum, Johannesburg	355
Second Floor Balcony: The Movie	245	The Gaze	357
The Listening Tour	248	Johnnie Sits Down	358
Home	251	Ring of Fire	361
Some Kind of Son	253	The Hair in my Life	363
Portrait of the Author as a Driven Man	265	The Bridge	365
Cloudless Day, Entebbe	267	To the Land of Endless Wanting	369
Stairway to Heaven	269		
Invasion of the Land Prawns	273	Afterwards	376
Trans-Uganda Sutra	295	Acknowledgments	381
Simba's Kapchorwa by Night	299		
The Big Dog Comes to the Village	305		

Going Into Uganda Time

In early 2008 I started doing something. At first, I didn't know exactly what I was doing or why I was doing it. But as the months of that year led from one to the next, both the what and the why began slowly coming into view.

What I was doing was getting rid of everything I owned. The reason was that I no longer wanted so many things to look after; it had become clear to me that it was time to move on — in every way possible. Decisions sometimes make themselves before we are consciously aware of the shift going on within. That's what was happening to me in early 2008. The process began unconsciously, and when the conscious mind caught up, it accelerated. I got rid of virtually everything in my wonderful old 1916 two-bedroom house on a pleasant street in a California town: the carpets, the hundreds of books and CDs and DVDs, the TV, the stereo, the art, the small treasures and collections, the chairs, the tables, the bed, the potted plants, the antique dresser and mirror, the utensils, the pots and pans, the washer and dryer, the hand tools, the power tools, all the extra clothing, and so on. Then I sold the house. Then I gave away the car.

As it would turn out, I was headed to Africa, but I had no clue of that until much later.

From beginning to end, the jettisoning of everything I owned took about a year and a half. I sold some of the stuff, but most I gave away — not out of generosity, but because I thought it to be the most expedient means of ridding myself of the many possessions I had accumulated over a half a century, most of which I no longer had any attachment to. As it happens, it is tougher to give away things than you might think, especially, I suspect, in the U.S. where things and ownership are exalted. Many times, as I handed over a framed artwork or, say, a chair or a carpet, the recipient would tell me, "Well, you can have it back if you want it."

"No," I'd say. "I won't want it back. I'm done with it." And, as I write this, nearly five years later, that is still the case.

There was nothing noble or selfless about my de-acquisitioning campaign. Indeed, it was self-serving. I was ready to make a change, and I wanted to do so quickly and with a minimum of baggage of any kind. When I travel I take as little with me as possible. Not because I'm committed to austerity or self-denial (on the contrary), but because I don't want much to carry.

A year and a few months after the Great Shedding of Things began, I decided to join the U.S. Peace Corps — at age 56. I don't recall where the idea came from, but once it popped into my head it seemed the right thing to do at the right time, and I became very focused on it. Eight months later, in early August 2009, I boarded a plane that took me to Uganda, a place I knew almost nothing about; I had never been there nor anywhere else in Africa. However, I was not alone in my ignorance. Few people in the U.S. know much about Uganda apart from the clichés (Amin, gorillas, Ebola), nor the rest of Africa. Africa is immense and unknowable. That's part of its appeal, its seductiveness, and what makes it endlessly fascinating. On balance, most Africans that I've met know little about the United States.

Speaking of immensity, just how big is Africa? Well, it's mind-blowingly big. You don't get a good sense of Africa's size by looking at a map or a globe, because the Mercator projection employed to make modern maps distorts the relative size of the continents and countries. Take a look at a world map. Greenland and Africa appear to be roughly the same size. In fact, Africa is 14 times larger than Greenland. You can fit the continental United States, China, Western Europe, Eastern Europe, Mexico, Iberia and India into Africa and, when you include the East African island nation of Madagascar, you can also squeeze in Japan. Africa is humongous.

Uganda, on the other hand is small, about the size of the state of Oregon. Yet, as of late 2012, Uganda's population was nearly 35 million, whereas Oregon's population was just under 4 million. There are numerous other differences between the two places that I won't detail here.

Even on the post-midnight drive from Entebbe airport to nearby Lweza where I stayed for the first few nights, the people were what I first noticed. They were everywhere. Many of them. Doing many things. People crowded the roadsides, walking home or away from home. There were people in huts, in shops, on bicycles, on motorcycles, leaning against trees, in bars and cafes; people around fires, working on cars, laughing, arguing, sweeping and washing, cooking and eating. And it doesn't change much when you get upcountry. There are still people everywhere. On many occasions, once I was living in rural Uganda, I'd hike into an area that I assumed was remote, isolated, relatively unpopulated. I'd hike for hours, only to come around a turn on a narrow trail and find dozens of people having a meal or working or just sitting and talking. They were always happy to see me and inevitably asked me to join them.

Ugandans are not merely friendly, they are preternaturally friendly. The vast majority are also charming, generous, great talkers, insightful, warm, handsome, beautiful, gracious, caring, stoic, even-tempered, welcoming, guileless, fine dancers, lovers of laughter and a hell of a lot of fun. These traits make the fact that there are so damn many of them packed onto a comparatively small piece of land much easier to take.

After arriving in Uganda, I spent several weeks living near Kampala with a family of 13, terrific folks whom I really enjoyed. Then I moved 6-7 hours' drive across the country to the Rwenzori Mountains village of Kyarumba, located in the far west, about 20 miles from Uganda's border with the Democratic Republic of Congo (DRC). It was there that I lived and worked for the next two-and-a-half years.

The clan in that mountain region is the Bukonzo, which is sometimes spelled Bakonzo or Bakonjo. The plural is Mukonzo or Mukonjo. Just to make things more confusing, the language is Lhukonzo, one of more than 50 clan languages in Uganda; the local languages can change every 50-60 miles. Between 600,000 and 700,000 people in western Uganda and the eastern DRC speak Lhukonzo as their native language. Like many African languages, there is no set orthography for Lhukonzo, so variant spellings and pronunciations are common. Other names for the language include Konjo, Rukonjo, Olukonjo or Olukonzo. I found that it didn't really matter how I pronounced a word, someone would correct me. It never failed.

I made little headway learning Lhukonzo. I don't have an ear for languages and, in my own defense, even other Ugandans acknowledge that it's a tough language to learn. But I learned basic greetings and developed a fondness for Lhukonzo's many beautiful words, such as wamatoka (you're noisy) and the magnificent omwankyajankyaja, of which I'll say more later.

After I'd been in Uganda a few months, an American friend of mine who's lived in Mexico for the last quarter-century sent me an email, "I'm happy that you are getting to experience having a love affair with another country," he wrote. I hadn't thought of my growing affection for the place in quite that way, but he was right. It was the beginning of a love affair.

Like any place (or lover), Uganda has its shortcomings, its unlovable characteristics, and you will come across some of them here, but not many. In any case, that is not what I chose to dwell on, and its less than admirable traits were not something I came across very often. Besides — with places as with people — when the good outweighs the bad by a great margin, one forgives.

What follows, then, is an account of love as it was beginning, seen with all the clarity with which a lover sees. This is not journalism, nor documentary. These words and images are utterly subjective, a very personal view of a place, its culture, its land, its people; what it felt and looked like as I became intoxicated by attraction. This is a portrait of a love affair, one that continues to this day.

Douglas Cruickshank

A Sixth Sense

OWEN EDWARDS

A well-traveled photographer once told me that 98 percent of what it takes to make good pictures in unfamiliar places is just being there. At the time, I thought this was false modesty, since he was quite famous. And I thought that "being there" really meant getting there, which is not always easy in out-of-the-way parts of the planet. In the years since hearing this, however, I've come to suspect that what he really meant was something deeper than trekking up mountains, across deserts, or through jungles. Rather, his hard-earned understanding was that to get good photographs, you have to be where you are, when you are there, with your eyes and your camera focused entirely on what's around you.

If this sounds like common sense — or common Zen — it is not something that necessarily comes naturally to most of us. And there are plenty of photographers, professionals who make a living at the trade, who would rather create their own environments in the controllable confines of a studio than go out to new territory and try to bring back visual impressions that are more memorable and revealing than glorified vacation snapshots. Seeing — entirely and intensely — the where and when and who of a place is the alchemist's ability needed for the best photography of new worlds. Douglas Cruickshank has this ability, first to connect emotionally, then to collect visually. The portraits and landscapes he made during a prolonged stay in the highlands of Uganda represent the keen-eyed but deeply affectionate impressions of an enchanted traveler.

Fair warning: Doug is a friend of mine. Therefore, to the untrusting, I may not be entirely dependable as a judge of his photography. But there's an important detail: His photographs were what launched our friendship; our friendship isn't the reason for my enthusiasm for his work. A few years ago, Doug and I were colleagues at a nonprofit educational foundation located on a beautiful ranch in Marin County, Calif. One day, soon after he came to the foundation, as I walked by his desk, I noticed a small, elegantly composed photo of an old tree trunk. I was impressed, and asked who had made it. The photographer was Doug himself, it turned out, and I asked if he had other pictures. (Old photography critics never quite turn in their badges.) Not long after that, I went to a small show of landscapes Doug had made on the Point Reyes National Seashore. I saw a wall full of extraordinary pictures, and ended up buying most of them. What was instantly apparent was that Doug saw photographs where it seemed there were no photographs, and, with imaginative, unexpected composition, he made them visible for us. His landscapes are anti-clichés, unique and visually counterintuitive, more in the tradition of Lee Friedlander than Ansel Adams. Walking miles through the remarkably varied topography of Point Reyes, he was able to

reveal the kinds of rhythms and counterpoint that many photographers miss as they look for the obviously photogenic great blue herons and coastal redwoods. Doug was able to find aesthetic order in nature's apparent chaos, yet without ever forcing nature to dance to his artistic tune. His landscapes, while sensuously pleasing, were also subtle tutorials in the act of looking, urging us to see what we were missing.

When Doug left Northern California toward the end of the summer of 2009 for Uganda, I assumed that what would surely be a gain for those he went to help would be a loss for his photography; so while I admired his decision, as an admirer of his work I felt especially sorry to see him go.

As it turns out, and as the photographs in this book vividly show, I had no reason to worry. What I understood about Doug on seeing his Point Reyes work is that he has an acute sixth sense … the sense of place. And what I would come to realize before he'd been in Africa for very long is that this sixth sense is a movable feast. So by the time he had settled into his coffee-growing village in the foothills of the Rwenzori Mountains, Doug was using his camera to show those of us who went to his website what he was seeing. And what he was seeing, along with gorillas, lions and landscapes, were the people he now lived among. In quick order, Doug became the unofficial town photographer of Kyarumba, Uganda.

Doug tells of a friend writing to him that he seemed to be having a love affair with the place, and his photographs prove this description accurate. In the literal, Elizabethan sense of characters in "The Tempest" or "A Midsummer's Night's Dream," he was charmed. While the pictures are an accurate record of a time and a place and one man's delighted curiosity, they are not journalism, which might require a certain distance and objectivity. The lack of journalism's idealized cool remove is, in fact, one of the many graces of the work, because the soul of the pictures is pure, familial affection, and a sense that this place is special.

Though he carried his camera everywhere and made pictures of the land and animals from domestic goats to lions, Doug's portraits of people — very different from his previous Point Reyes work — have the kind of relaxed intimacy that normally can only be found in pictures made by a neighbor of neighbors, or by a family member. Doug is a friendly, avuncular presence, and it may be that he was accepted after a while as everyone's kind uncle, toting a camera around town as he walked back and forth between his house and his work.

These everyday walks could bring photographic serendipity. One day, for instance, just ahead of him, a gaggle of young girls in brightly colored cotton dresses meandered along, in no hurry. To get them to move a little faster, Doug playfully stamped his foot. The girls rushed ahead like startled birds, giggling, and then slowed again to their leisurely pace. Another stamp of the foot, another burst of temporary speed, another slowing, until an impromptu game was born. When the girls came to a log bridge over a stream, Doug shouted that he wanted to take their picture. With no further prompting, they turned and waved, like the happy cast members of a successful play acknowledging the applause of an enthusiastic audience. The photo that captured this moment of spontaneous joy (p. 366) reflects all the sweetness that made Doug fall in love with the village and his neighbors.

Another, larger gathering of schoolchildren, in two groups on a grassy slope with a misty valley in the background, gives us a slightly mysterious look at what must be a large share of the young kids in the area. Why they are there, in two formations — one group, mostly boys, in a more-or-less straight line, the other, mostly girls, in an imperfect V, like geese on their first migration — is unexplained. It's as if they have been collected for a class picture, with the town photographer brought in to stop time for posterity's sake. At the point of the V, three girls draw the eye. One, in a long, gray dress, is very serious looking, and stares intently at the photographer. Just behind her, another girl is equally serious, equally unsure about the enterprise. The third, in bright yellow, looks off defiantly to one side, arms crossed, all attitude, clearly not to be intimidated or made to strike a "nice girl" pose. If you think back to your grade school days, this is a classmate you definitely don't want to get on the wrong side of.

There are few if any pictures in this book that don't evoke pleasure with a good long look. But the portraits Doug made of his fellow villagers are special … an admiring album of friends and the children of friends. Though most of the portraits are done straight on, with the subjects striking their own poses, there is a satisfying variety in the pictures. In photographs of couples, while the men are often soberly dressed, in jackets and suits that may first have been worn by office workers in Europe and America, the women are adorned with an amazing array of brightly printed cottons. There are odd and intriguing little mysteries in some of the pictures. In one (p. 110), three men stand behind three seated women; the men stare straight at the camera, but the women, far more interested in something happening — we have no idea what — offstage right, pay no attention to the local photographer (by now, no doubt, a quotidian presence).

In another (p. 37), two boys, possibly brothers, stand attentively for their picture, one wearing a small cross on a chain around his neck, the other in a sweat shirt with an incongruous plaid Scotch terrier sewn on the chest. Behind the pair is a small, Barbie-type doll, stuck to the wall for some entirely unexplainable reason.

For a photographer, the best sort of "being there" is being there — wherever — for long enough to blend in, to witness the everydayness of the locals and, as E.M. Forster urged, "only connect." In more than two years in the village, Doug saw all the shades of life there. One great example of his honorary villager status is a wedding scene — a photograph (p. 345) where Doug seems so much a part of the crowd that no one seems aware of the man with the camera. The bride, a large young woman in an elaborate off-the-shoulder white dress, seems possibly to be the least happy person in the picture, as if she's having serious doubts about the ritual in which she is the main attraction. All around her are bridesmaids in matching dresses, a self-assured woman in blue who may be the maid of honor, and friends who seem to be enjoying themselves enormously. Far in the back of the crowd is that wonderfully peculiar touch that adds an unforgettable element to the picture: Standing in the bed of a pickup truck, a woman in bright orange clutches an electric bass guitar and seems to be singing at the top of her lungs. Like a drawing by Saul Steinberg, the photograph keeps revealing delightful details and telling a more and more complex story the longer you look at it.

One of the aspects of Doug's Point Reyes landscapes that appeals to me is the plangent sense both of time captured and of time passing. Ancient, sea-worn rocks and wind-felled trees have a haunting beauty, at once melancholy and reassuring: All things come to an end, but nature goes on. A similar resonance can be felt in many of the photographs Doug made on trips to the ancient island of Zanzibar (pp. 306-325), once a British protectorate and now a semi-autonomous region of Tanzania. Though no longer the elegant metropolis it was in its heyday as a spice trading port, past glory echoes in the ruins of the palaces of merchant princes and various trading and colonial powers, from Persia to England. Among these ruins, Doug revived the cooler, more contemplative formal style of his California photographs. For instance, in an image (p. 319) in which the pale green and pale blue of the Indian Ocean and sky are partly framed by a suspended stone balustrade once attached to a house long since devoured by years and tides, the constancy of the land and sea underscored by the entropy that stalks all paths of glory. It ought to be a composition in a minor key, but somehow it strikes a sweeter chord in the viewer. In this viewer, at least.

Picking favorites images from such an endearing, enduring collection is neither easy nor, for a veteran critic, entirely proper. But I can't resist pointing out a particular portrait that seems to embody perfectly the sweetness of the people Doug found himself among, and the embrace of the place he so clearly fell in love with. A young boy, perhaps 6 or 7, with enormous dark eyes and a slightly shy expression, has stuck a picture of a soccer star to his forehead, a kind of votive to display to all his bond with his hero. This boy, and this photograph, are not to be resisted. Like so many of the pictures in this book, the portrait tells us that a man who went off to be a stranger in a strange land ended up right at home, among friends, after all.

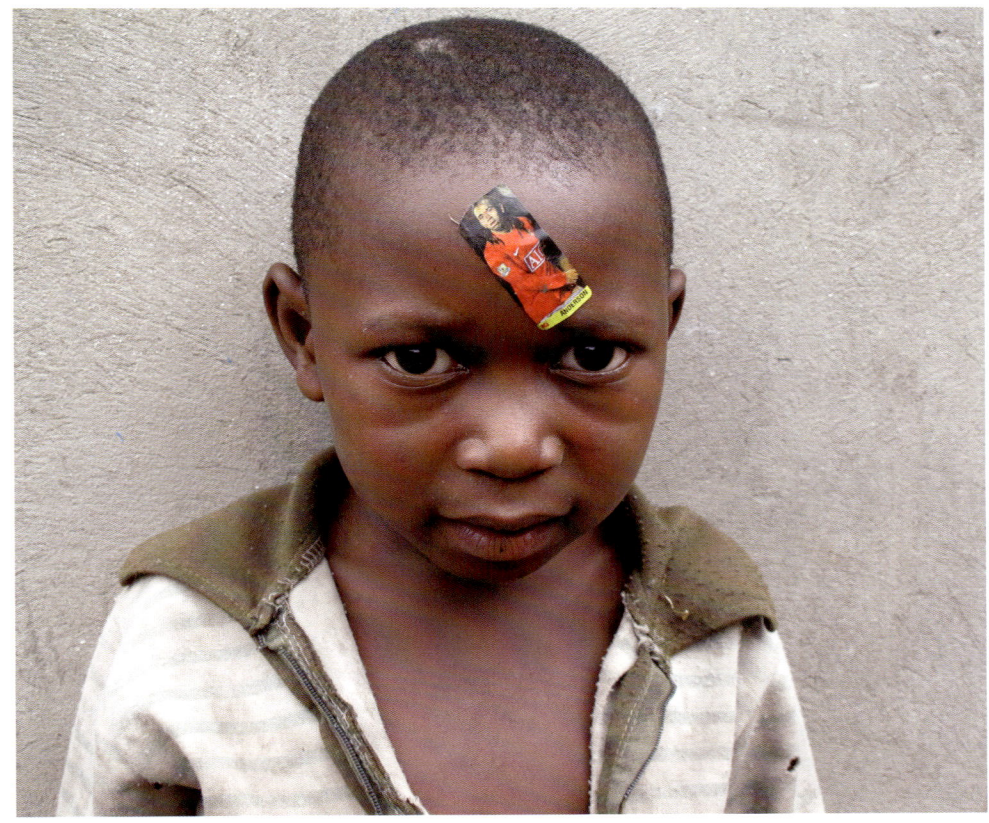

SOMEHOW
Living on Uganda Time

3 NOVEMBER 2009

Omwanjakyanjakya

This is where the world began and that is the first tree, tree No. 1. Rather, that is where morning began. Actually, that is where my morning began, most mornings. It's where I stood, the view I saw, when the burning sun emerged dripping wet from Lake Victoria and painted this skyscraper tree with mango light. And I always stopped and looked at it and the people, many of them children, carrying their 20-liter jerri cans to and from the village borehole, the only source of water for most of them.

I then continued down the path to the right of the tree, a shortcut past brush, under another tree filled with ornament-like weaver bird nests, around palms and small garden plots, up and over a creek or two, the usual cows and goats straining at tie ropes, and "Good morning, Ssebo," from uniformed boys and girls on their way to school. Thirty minutes or so of walking brought me to the place I spent my days for a few weeks. At night, I returned home via the same route and tree No. 1 had become an umbrella, a refuge from the crying sky, or the cloudy-soft light of African moonbeams, the glare of Jupiter, and the spray of the Milky Way.

As for that word up there at the top, the one that won't stop — *omwanjakyanjakya* — it means "morning" in Lhukonzo, the language I'm learning, or would be learning if I had a memory and if my 56-year-old palate could be reformed so that it could make the sounds that only native Lhukonzo speakers can make. Still, I'm slowly, slowly becoming able to produce an unreasonable facsimile of this language, which a patient, tolerant and imaginative Lhukonzo speaker may be able to make sense of if she's in the mood, if the winds are right, if the rain comes and the leaves blow, and the planets align.

Omwanjakyanjakya: Not as impossible to pronounce as it looks — once you learn that "ky" in Lhukonzo is pronounced as "ch" is in English words like church and cheese. Then just disassemble that elephantine word into its six syllables:
1. **Om** – like the spiritual chant
2. **wan** – like wand without the d
3. **ja** – like jaw
4. **kyan** – like John, but with the ch sound
5. **ja** – once more, because you need two jaws
6. **kya** – as in the dance, Cha, cha, cha

Then run them all together, fast as a black mamba, the fastest snake on earth, clocked, some say, pursuing prey at 12 mph, maybe faster.

Fortunately, though black mambas live here in Uganda, they are shy and elusive and I'll almost certainly never see one — unless it sees me first, in which case you'll be hearing the story from someone else. But if the dark and unlikely should occur, it would have a bright side. There are worse ways to go than the last word you hear being the world's swiftest serpent whispering, "Omwanjakyanjakya."

3 NOVEMBER 2009

The War of the Angels in the Days of Rain

They are not angels by most people's definition, though they look like they could dance on the head of a pin. They're termites, or white ants, as the locals call them. They build the big, conical, rust-colored mounds that punctuate the countryside around here. In any case, something (the ferocious rain, perhaps, or a testy god) removed the small creatures' tiny, silvery, oblong wings and sprinkled them over the ground; they were everywhere underfoot this morning. The red dirt resembled a field after battle, all that remained following the clash of a miniature flying infantry: the War of the Angels.

There was a light rain falling as I walked and the clouds, remnants of the storm, were skulking off to water the rest of the country. Two boys passed me on the path and I greeted them. One turned to me, reached in a plastic bag he was carrying, and offered a palmful of roasted termites. I took them and ate them. They tasted like small almonds with feet. The wet season has evidently arrived, albeit some weeks late — good news for everyone except the termites.

5 NOVEMBER 2009

The Invisible Dog Choir

My first night here, staying on the outskirts of Kampala, I was introduced to the musical stylings of the Uganda Philharmonic Dog Choir. You rarely see dogs here. They're invisible, and the ones you do see are so skinny they're becoming invisible. People don't keep them as pets; they keep them as guards and only let them out at night. And when night falls, the pups are ready to rock.

At about 1 A.M. the UPDC started tuning up. They seemed to be in top form almost instantly, thanks to their many long nights of practice. They may not have been staying strictly in tune, but their projection was excellent and they burned with passion. The first howl went up right under my window and then, like a precision relay, the song passed from hilltop to hilltop, alley to alley, tin roof to tin roof. An exquisite fading echoplex effect was produced as every hound from Kampala to Khartoum joined the choir. The howls drifted into the distance in every direction — north toward Sudan, east to Kenya, west to the Congo, south toward Rwanda and Tanzania. Then, after a moment of near silence, back came the sonic chant, galloping like a pack of running dogs, until the Pavarotti of canines under my window let rip with a joyous caterwaul that must have shaken the monkeys out of the jackfruit trees.

My ear is not what it once was, but I believe the UPDC was attempting a Bach chorale piece that enchanted evening, though it could have been "In-A-Gadda-Da-Vida." Whatever. It doesn't really matter. It was stunning, and the effect — a complex layering of discord and harmony, love and angst, heart and hellraising — had all the ethereal transcendence of a heavenly pond of fur-bearing bullfrogs laying it down for the gods, for eternity, and for music-starved insomniacs everywhere.

8 NOVEMBER 2009

Coming Into Tombstone

Going down the long, wide, cinnamon road into town, a straightaway stretches out ahead. A bulging cloud the color of wet cement pushes the wind directly toward me, kicking up orange dust as it comes. The first big drops of rain dot the ground. The low buildings on either side of the road, the cattle wandering alongside the people, the goats, the chickens, all make it look like I'm approaching Tombstone, Arizona, 1880.

Way up ahead, emerging from the rusty powder, four exclamation marks are being propelled by the hot breeze and their own slow, gentle movements. All are dressed in long gowns. Two are in black (one of those is wearing a crimson turban), one is in dark green and one wears cerise. The fabric flutters and dances around them. They walk with the same easy lilt and rhythm as laundry on the line, moving with the air.

The ongoing, ever-changing street scenes here could be right out of Our Town, Uganda: a Thornton Wilder vision filtered through the decades of Obote, Amin, Obote II and Museveni, with set designs by an African Currier & Ives, complete with young boy, stick in hand, chasing a hoop, though in this case it's a length of sugar cane and a cast-off boda-boda tire.

8 NOVEMBER 2009

Names

People here seem to match their children's names, the so-called Christian names, to the outsize drama of the place, its landscape, history, weather, wildness, mythology and spirituality — both indigenous and adopted. The African names are no less charged (if anything, they are more so), but the religious, frequently biblical, connection of the others is a constant reminder of how the people of this often theatrical land see, or wish to see, their roles. I've met Samson, Israel, Daniel, Judith, Joseph, Esther, James, Isaac, Ruth, Joshua, Elijah, numerous Marys and Graces, a Govinda and an Omega. And Maurice.

The first Sunday I was here in the village, I was standing outside the church and an elderly man walked up to me, nodded and sat down on the large boulder I was standing next to. Someone had applied a spray-paint stencil to the boulder. Its silvery block letters read: "Jesus Lives." The man told me he'd been a driver for the hospital a few miles from here for 25 years, but had to retire after his eyes were damaged by looking at the flame of a welding torch. He said, "I was blinded by the light," and laughed a little. He seemed almost amused by his misfortune.

Motioning toward the nearby Rwenzori Mountains — the Mountains of the Moon — he told me he remembered when they had much more snow on them. "But now we have the climate changing," he said. We talked for a while longer. He pointed out the location of his house, spoke of his many children, greeted arriving churchgoers by waving his cane at them. I told him where I was from and why I was living here, and I belatedly introduced myself. "Ah," he said, "and my name is Lazarus."

8 NOVEMBER 2009

Pterodactyls to Watch Over Us

Sulky, petulant or merely resigned? It's hard to get a good read on their attitude, but they're inarguably eerie, magisterial and frickin' strange. They are also immense, have long, bandy legs, bald, scab-encrusted heads, and they possess the singular trait that always cries out, "Hug me!": They eat carrion, and most anything else that will fit in their enormous beaks. And then there are the pinkish, pendulous air sacs that droop from their backs and throats. But why dwell on those? We all have certain features we'd just as soon others ignored. Once airborne, however, they have the grace and control of Nureyev, and their performances are nearly as hypnotic to watch. They are difficult to love, but love them I do. Even their Latin species name is appealing in a gawky, homely sort of way: *Leptoptilos crumeniferus*.

Resembling creatures out of science fiction (they should have been in "Blade Runner"), or prehistory, Marabou storks operate constant high-altitude surveillance flights over Kampala or stand in open lots and on building ledges, glowering at all before them. They are some of the largest birds on the planet. Held aloft by their massive wings that can span more than 9 feet, they trace circles and ovals and figure eights high over the mad megalopolis, and come in on long, sloping descents to the tops of trees, cellphone towers, billboards. Imagine if L.A., New York, London or Berlin had hundreds of pterodactyls regularly patrolling overhead, and you've got a picture of what Kampala air traffic looks like any day of the week.

There is something inscrutable and otherworldly about them. They're also mildly menacing (a mature male is nearly 5 feet tall), especially if you're nearby when they land or are walking close by when they're bickering with one another. They are the overlords from some distant, conquering planet, an occupying army of guardian soldiers sent here to watch over us — firm but benign until orders arrive from their faraway home to be otherwise.

The other day, I was sitting in a taxi in Kampala in the usual gridlock, but I lucked out by being frozen in time and carbon monoxide near a median strip planted with two jacaranda trees, which three mama storks had chosen as an ideal place to raise up their young ones. I was entertained (if that's the appropriate word) trying to figure out exactly what the furry, dripping, meaty chunks were that the doting mamas were delivering to their demanding offspring. The noise the storklets made as their food flew in was like the soundtrack to a horror movie, but the looks on the moms' long faces as the little nippers gobbled their breakfast was as heartwarming as a Gerber commercial.

10 NOVEMBER 2009

African Taxi Opera

Who knew it would be so easy to catch a taxi in the middle of Africa? Not in a city, not even in a town, but in a village, a small village up in the mountains, literally at the end of the road. For that matter, you can just hang by the side of the highway out in the middle of Nowheresville and a taxi will be by in a matter of minutes. And if there's any way the driver feels he can bend the laws of physics to squeeze in one more person, you've got a ride. People are astonishingly tolerant about, say, having a 56-year-old muzungu cram himself into an already overstuffed back seat and sit on their laps. In turn, I've had several people sit on me. You get used to it.

There are taxis all over the place. People have to get from here to there, and hardly anyone owns a vehicle (unless you're a muckety-muck working for the U.N., UNICEF, Save the Children, CARE, Peace Corps, etc., in which case you're chauffeured around in a ginormous, sparkly new SUV with your org's logo plastered on the sides). The boda-bodas — motorcycle taxis — are another story. You ride those for one of five reasons:

1. You have absolutely no alternative and you feel it's a good day to die (or be maimed);
2. You're young enough that you've yet to be convinced of the whole mortality thing;
3. You're psychotic;
4. You wish to become psychotic;
5. Did I already mention you feel it's a good day to die?

The automobile taxis are only marginally safer.

Anyway, getting a taxi here is not much of a problem. But getting in the taxi can be. Exiting can also be a challenge. The other day I was in a town about an hour away from my home, so I went to where the taxis were massing and had an amiable, albeit lengthy, argument with eight or 10 drivers, simultaneously, about what would be a reasonable fee for being taken to the outer limits of human endurance while at the same time being moved closer to my home at a speed of 80 to 90 miles per hour (dropping to a leisurely 75 to avoid goats and cattle), during which I'd be as close as one can get to another person or persons without actually impregnating them. We settled on 4,000 shillings, about $2.

The arrangement inside the chariot I chose — an 1851 model Toyota Corolla that had seen action in the Crimean War — rivaled the stateroom scene in the Marx Brothers' "A Night at the Opera," one of the finest bits those great saints of surrealism ever captured on film. (I'm sure it's on YouTube. Stop reading this and go find it immediately.) Crammed in the back seat were four women, two babies and a toddler. One woman held a bag of charcoal on her lap. Really. And three men, one of whom was me — 6-foot-1, 200+ pounds — were in front. Cool, let's roll.

The driver starts the car and aims it toward our destination. And off we go. For about a block. Because you need gas to go on an hour's drive, don't you? Yes, of course, so let's go find a gas station. But wait. Let's try to get the radio tuned in first. Never mind, it won't tune in, so we'll just turn the volume way up instead. Is it me or is it so hot in here we could all pass out in a matter of minutes? Windows down? No, only the driver's window goes down. The rest have been stuck closed since the Crimean unpleasantness. Actually, "Rhinestone Cowboy" sounds better filtered through a thick layer of static. Turn it up more – good idea. OK, we're gassed up, let's hit it! Is that a reggae version of "Ode to Billie Joe"? Can't tell, let's turn up the radio some more. No, I'm pretty sure it's UB40's cover of "I Got You Babe." Oops, one of the babies just got sick. I don't know why. The interior temperature is only 134 degrees and the 18 percent of the exhaust that's not getting sucked into the passenger compartment is going right out the tailpipe. Kid's no trouper. Don't coddle him. Better yet, pass him up here, cause we're picking up one more guy (I swear) and he can hold the li'l fussbudget. Which he does — turns out he's the father.

We finally did get underway, but things went like that for the entire trip. At one point a huge baboon ran across the road on his way to plunder a maize field, but for some reason those in the car who were still conscious paid little attention.

13 NOVEMBER 2009

Vaches Sans Frontières

In his masterly book "Africa: Altered States, Ordinary Miracles," Richard Dowden says the cattle here, known as Ankole or Ankole-Watusi, are direct descendents of the ones pictured in Egyptian art from the time of the pharaohs. And the cows seem to know it. They've got some major attitude working. I suppose it's what gets them through. Being a cow in Africa is a tough gig. In any case, they go where they will and they go there at whatever speed they choose to. ("Honk, honk! Can we get around, please. You're blocking the road with your humongous slow-moving cow bodies." "No, you can't get around please. You can bloody well wait until we find some foliage that we deem suitable to dine on. Honk all the f*ck you want, wanker!")

But then who wouldn't be high on themselves with that lineage? Not to mention their stunning good looks: They sport horns that resemble a matched set of Brancusi's "Bird in Space," only bent -- a rack that makes the bodacious antennae on Texas Longhorns look wimpy by comparison. What must it do to your head to grow those damn things, and to your neck to hold them up all day? From the shoulders forward the Ankole are the ne plus ultra of bovine structural engineering. In the other direction they're, well, cows.

One of my deep pleasures the first 10 weeks I was here was sitting on the front porch of the family home where I was staying and watching the fashion parade of humans and animals at the end of the day. It was visually delicious, funny, poignant, amazing, shocking — sometimes all of that at once.

Here comes a woman wearing a long black dress and a bright red head wrap, the end of which tumbles down her back. On her chest is an oversize white cross that appears to be made of ivory. On her shoulder, she's carrying a large, cylindrical grinding bowl made of wood, with the pestle balanced inside. She's followed by a boy urging six cows down the road while talking on his cellphone. He has a jackfruit on his head. A linen merchant is also doing a balancing act, but he's holding an 18-inch-high stack of his neatly folded merchandise -- sheets with a floral print. A man has a pole resting across his shoulders hung with bras of various sizes and colors. He's selling them door to door. A woman is holding a large chunk of pineapple wrapped in a banana leaf (Ugandan pineapple is 10 times sweeter and juicier than any other). There's a machete balanced on her head. Another woman passes — she's Muslim — wearing a white calf-length gown with white satin pants underneath, a black shawl over her shoulders, and a white turban-like head wrap. Flocks of children go by intermittently and yell to me: "Hi, muzungu!" or "See you!" Miscellaneous cows, goats and chickens wander aimlessly, nonplussed by the human splendor around them, window shopping for snacks that strike their fancy.

Speaking of which, my favorite parade participants were four of my neighbors who happened to be Ankole cattle — two calves and their moms. They lived across the street in a small paddock. That's where they spent their nights anyway. Every morning, the local herdsmen would come collect the four and steer them to prime grazing land outside the village. Apparently, he provided this service — like a Manhattan dog walker — to several households. The foursome knew the drill: As soon as he let them out of their enclosure in the morning, they trotted cheerfully off to breakfast, herdsman running alongside. But dusk was when I set my watch by them. As I sat on the porch taking in the endlessly surprising procession, the two cows and two calves would come strolling down the road, single file, unaccompanied, knowing exactly where they were headed, always punctual, walk under the laundry line and between two adobe buildings, and through the gate of the paddock the four of them could just barely fit into -- to wait patiently as the moon rose and set, and the sun slipped up over the horizon and made it morning, so they could follow their herdsman and their happy routine one more time.

15 NOVEMBER 2009

Behold the Blue-Headed Stranger

We tremble before his magnificence, we are awed by his extravagance, his polychrome flamboyance makes the stage regalia of Elton John, Liberace, Cher, Elvis, Patti LaBelle and David Bowie seem drab and dreary by comparison. One's first sighting of a blue-headed agama is startling to an almost psychedelic degree. Is this a flashback? (No such luck.) Will this hallucinatory reptile now stand on its brilliant cobalt blue tail and address me in Latin? Or am I looking at a computer graphic concoction that has slipped its tether and leapt from the digital universe into this one?

It must be a good omen, or maybe he heard me call his name. While typing this, I glance at the wall outside my office doorway. Sitting atop it, gazing out at the steep hillside, is a pensive blue-headed agama. I see two or three a day around here. By the look on his face he's either wondering where best to start when solving the problems of the universe or he's interested in gobbling the line of ants marching up the wall. It's difficult to be sure which. He's a big brute: 14 to 16 inches long from the tip of his fashionable tail to his handsome, true-blue snout. I approach him. He keeps one eye on me and the other on the ants. Occasionally he pops one in his mouth the way I used to eat Junior Mints at the movies. I watch him, he watches me, I creep closer. He's an eyeful. Then, like a man forced to leave a banquet at the first course, he takes a last sorrowful glance at the ants and disappears over the wall.

17 NOVEMBER 2009

A Faint Recollection

Life came to a brief halt for a few minutes. No, it was more like a rolling stall. I went to another world and came back. I was falling, and I was on the edge of a very high, steep hill. Time stopped. Just briefly. Only for me. Not for long. I think that's what happened. If memory serves.

There I was at the top of the hill, which I had just hiked up quickly in intense heat. I'd been keeping up, more or less, with a 28-year-old who's been climbing the hills around here since he was a pup. I'd had a minor stomach bug the night before, but I was ignoring the lingering effects. I'd had a very light breakfast — a banana or two — and no lunch. By the time we reached the summit, I was in a lather. My shirt and pants were nearly soaked through. I looked like I'd been holding my head under a shower. I squatted down on the edge of the hilltop to cool off, catch my breath. I stood up, leaned against a tree, looked way, way down to the village we'd come from. Amazing how the earth turns; you can see it. It feels strange.

The tree began to dance with me. It wanted to lead. I followed. The tree had two left feet and so did I. We staggered and stumbled as a gathering went on nearby, people I'd known for years in the states, chatting in groups of two and three in a suburban American backyard. It was an afternoon barbeque or a party. Then, as the tree let me slip from its arms, someone caught me; I couldn't catch myself. I was just about to hit the ground and a friend ran over, held me up. As quickly as I'd gone, I was back, high on an African hilltop, outside an adobe church, the hills of the Congo visible just a few miles to the west.

The blood finally got to my brain, I guess. I sat for a bit, rested, came back to life. We ate lunch and I spoke to the group, then we walked down the very high, steep hill, while it rained and rained and rained and rained and rained.

19 NOVEMBER 2009

The Devil Drives

Starting in a hollowed log of wood – some thousand miles up a river, with an infinitesimal prospect of returning! I ask myself, "Why?" and the only echo is "damned fool! … the Devil drives."
– Sir Richard Francis Burton

"My poor body, madam, requires it: I am driven on by the flesh; and he must needs go that the devil drives."
– All's Well that Ends Well

"Needs go" is not a phrase that gets trotted out much anymore, not around here anyway, but it had its day, and Google, whose long, digital tentacles even reach my two rooms near the Mountains of the Moon, reveals that it means "necessity compels" – by some preternatural force, perhaps, which is what the indefatigable Burton and his countryman, Willie the Shake (as Lord Buckley christened the Bard), were no doubt referring to.

What drives me everywhere here, however, is Moses, but he's not a devil, he's an angel full of grace and good cheer, and one hell of a driver. Moses the Intrepid, I call him. He Who Will Not Be Stopped.

Moses and his indestructible Toyota, which must have an oil pan carved from a single block of granite because we have slammed that thing on dozens of rocky roadbeds and goat trails and paths to who-knows-where and it has yet to spring a leak. Astonishing. Moses goes through mud holes that would bog down a cape buffalo or a Caterpillar tractor, but out we come on the other side. I shake my head or reach over and give him a single pat on the shoulder, and Moses just glances at me and smiles. Doubt? He doesn't know doubt. Fear? He laughs in the face of fear. Ruts, potholes, oncoming traffic? What ruts? What potholes? What oncoming traffic?

"Moses," I said the other day, as he smoothly negotiated a particularly treacherous dirt road that looked like it belonged in "The Wages of Fear" — it was barely clinging to an all but vertical hillside; the rain had reduced visibility to zero or less; a long eternity was just outside my fogged-up window — "given where you can get us in this beat-up jalopy, I think if you had a big, new SUV, you could drive to the top of Kilimanjaro!"

"I could do that," he said. "I could take us there."

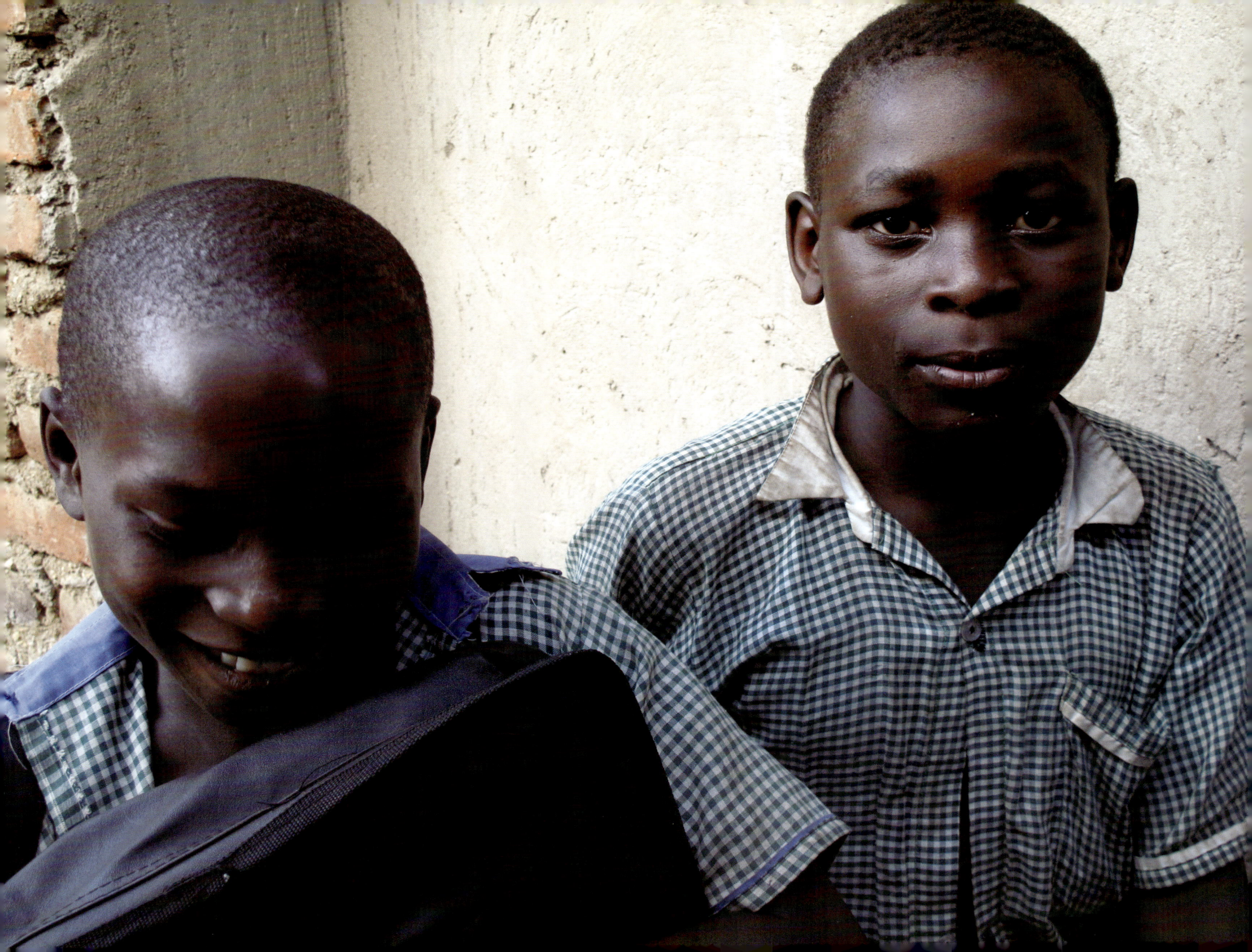

21 NOVEMBER 2009

What's That Sound, Elijah?

At first, he had no clue what it was. He reached up to touch it, though there was nothing to touch but some rushing air coming through my lips. Over time he became less concerned with figuring it out. He just listened. And dozed.

The first two-and-a-half months I was here I lived at a family home with six children, the oldest of whom was 12. The youngest was Elijah. He turned 4 months old a couple of weeks before I left. Even as mellow babies go, Elijah is a wee Buddha. He has his moments of caterwauling, but they're rare and brief. Mostly he just hangs out, watches, smiles his knowing-Buddha smile, rides around in the arms of whoever is holding him at the moment. Sometimes that was me. I considered it a challenge to see if, during the few moments a day he was out of sorts, I could get him to chill. The successful technique I used was discovered by accident.

I'm an inveterate whistler. I've been doing it for so long that I'm not even aware of it. So, when I'd walk Elijah up and down the back courtyard, ducking under the laundry lines, letting the shirts and sheets and socks brush over his round, brown face, or pace back and forth on the front lawn with him while watching the nightly procession of dramatically horned cows and extravagantly clothed people, I'd whistle. He put his small hand up to my mouth the first time, but after that he rested his head against my chest with that calm, utterly relaxed heaviness that only babies can achieve. I'd whistle "Skylark," "What a Difference a Day Makes," "Ain't Misbehavin'," the flute solo lead-in from the Blues Project's "Flute Thing." The idea was to soothe him and shape his taste at the same time.

It had an uncanny effect. After a few minutes of whistling, Elijah would be well within the city limits of Snoozeville. And then I'd hand him off to his mother or father and down for a nap he'd go. How pleasant was it for me? I didn't even mind the several times he urinated on my arm.

According to his mother, the aptly named Grace, my absence has not gone unnoticed by his roly-poly-ness. Not long after I relocated to the other side of the country, I got a late-night text message from her. I'm guessing she was up because Elijah was up and being very un-Buddha-like. Grace wrote me a single line that was the perfect motherly blend of sweetness, fatigue and desperation: "I think Elijah misses your whistling."

23 NOVEMBER 2009

Bicycle of Smoke

English is the official language here, but it's most people's second language. Ugandans grow up speaking their clan language at home and among extended family and friends. Luganda, native to central Uganda, is spoken by the largest number of people, but there are more than 50 indigenous languages in this country, a nation slightly smaller than the state of Oregon. In the west, where I'm living, Lhukonzo is one of several native tongues.

When speaking with Ugandans in English, it soon becomes clear that it's not American English that they're most familiar with. They hear it on TV and in movies, of course, and there are a fair number of Americans in Kampala, but once you're out in the country, you're a novelty, and even conversing with fluent English speakers is not the fluid trading of words you might have thought you'd be getting into.

Quickly, if you wish to be understood, you learn to slow down your speech, you avoid slang and jargon, you try to phrase things in clear, concise constructions – an especially good exercise for a writer. In other words, I speak the way I'd like to be spoken to (but rarely am) by Lhukonzo speakers. Years ago, when I was in Vietnam, I took a several-days-long drive up the Mekong Delta to the Cambodian border and back down to Ho Chi Minh City. At one point, when I was anxious to get rolling again after a lunch stop, I unthinkingly suggested to my driver and translator that we "hit the road." This remark was met with a deafening silence and a long and amusing discussion about American vernacular ensued. It took up much of an afternoon and came to a rousing if off-key climax with me singing "Hit the Road, Jack" to my two traveling companions.

Examples of the Ugandans' poetic approach to English and their naturally artful way with language, whether their own or adopted, reach my ears several times a day. This morning Rosalind's computer battery was running low and she explained to me that the machine was "complaining of having little fire." Another time, a local council leader was talking about the hard times of the past. Recalling those sad days, he said, "Poverty became a song everywhere."

My favorite meeting of English and Lhukonzo, however, is when "egali yomukyi," the Lhukonzo term for "train" (a vehicle that no longer exists in Uganda), is translated verbatim into English. The result: "bicycle of smoke."

26 NOVEMBER 2009

Bring It

Somewhere in the vast territory between joyous celebration and butt-numbing endurance marathon is an elaborate, noisy and altogether extraordinary event that makes the coronation of a king or the birthday party of a maharajah seem like a PTA meeting in Fresno. It is a Ugandan introduction ceremony. It's vaguely analogous to an engagement party in the states only more, way more.

I went as the guest of a Ugandan friend, Stephen, the uncle of the bride-to-be, Loda, who will marry Ben. And all day long, very long, Ben and Loda were as happy as I've ever seen two people be. Loda's father passed away a long time ago, so Stephen, who's in his early 60s, and his older brothers, Livingston, Robert and James, were the hosts (though the groom-to-be foots the bill). It was held at Robert's home in the lush country outside Kampala.

Open-sided tents were erected around a small, grassy area, which served as a stage and parade ground. I sat in the front row on the side directly across from Ben's family and friends. Next to me were Stephen, Livingston, Robert and James. There was a DJ torturing an eardrum-shattering sound system with a mix of traditional African music, hip-hop and insipid American pop, twinkly lights strung everywhere they should be and everywhere they could be, beautiful women and handsome men dressed as if they came from the place where dressing up was invented (they did), and so many giggly, fidgety, scampering, fascinated children, that it was hard to get anything approaching an accurate count. In the back, behind a fence, the caterer had been at it for more than a day before the guests arrived. The food crew, all dressed in matching orange T-shirts, labored over giant, steaming pots the size of California hot tubs, making matooke (mashed plantains), rice, potatoes, ground nut sauce, spiced chicken wrapped in banana leaves, goat and several other dishes I couldn't identify, pronounce or spell. The three cakes, two made to look like Ugandan pumpkins and one crafted to resemble a bowl of matooke covered with banana leaf, were made by a local cake artist.

As is the tradition, Ben and Loda's family each hired a professional speaker to speak for them. The speakers – shouters is more like it -- make a lot of money for their day's duty, and they earn it. They are a hybrid of evangelical preacher and boss jock bellower, crooner and carnival barker. They banter with one another, sing the glories of Ben and Loda; Ben's man promises that Ben will eternally worship Loda; Loda's man insists that Loda will love Ben longer than that. They plead the cases of their clients, they praise, they quip, they cajole, they go for cheap laughs, and they keep the crowd worked up for the entire afternoon and into the evening. It is a party-and-a-half, and another three-quarters after that.

It's called an introduction because it's the ceremony at which the man is formally introduced to the woman's family. (Of course, most of them have already met, probably years ago, but that's beside the

PHOTOGRAPHS ON PAGES 42, 44 AND 45 BY ISAAC KAWEESA

point.) Loda's sisters and nieces and aunts and brothers all introduce themselves to Ben and his family, and then Ben's family reverses the process. But it's not just, "Nice to meet you." First Loda's aunts on, say, her mother's side, dressed in extravagant matching gowns — the ones with the short, puffy sleeves and wide waist sashes that are favored for such occasions, and worn every day by many women, are known as gomasis — dance their way to the grassy stage in a line, then kneel on woven mats before Ben's family. One of the aunts, usually the oldest, says a few words of praise and welcome, and Ben's spokesman then walks out and gives each of them a small gift. Then another group, maybe Loda's aunts on her father's side, come shimmying to the center. Then Loda's brothers. Her nephews. Ben's uncles. It continues like that for hours and hours.

Finally, once that seemingly endless back and forth has run out of relatives to fuel it, it's time for Ben to deliver the goods. It's time for the dowry. Also known as the bride price, it's a source of growing controversy and newspaper editorials here, but it is still the centerpiece of introduction ceremonies, and despite calls for it to end, that doesn't seem likely to happen any time soon.

In any case, at the ceremony I attend, no one is objecting. It wouldn't do any good if they were. There's no stopping the long, snaking line of Ben's female friends and relatives that starts far beyond the curve of the road and is slowly, surely and rhythmically sauntering toward the ceremony. And each woman – there are 70 or more – is carrying something on her head. Even the wind and rain that's now moving in is not slowing their approach.

As the women get closer, I see they're carrying large baskets, each covered with white netting and tied with a wide chartreuse ribbon. They are for Loda or a member of Loda's family. The line gradually makes its way to the center of the crowd. In the baskets are fruit, vegetables, sugar, millet, laundry soap, other household powders, liquids and emollients, rice, salt, tea, coffee, ground nuts, margarine and loaves of bread.

Next come the men of Ben's entourage bringing with them large, 50-pound sacks of beans, maize flour, cassava flour, rice, huge bunches of green bananas, cases of Coke, Fanta Orange, Sprite, Mountain Dew, Pepsi and Rwenzori water. Four men using a wooden pallet as a platter carry in a full hind-quarter of beef, its hoof daintily hanging off one side. Then a living room-full of overstuffed couches and chairs is hefted in, along with a full set of luggage. Now the line of women reappears, slow-dancing down the red dirt road, each one carrying a large rectangular box wrapped in crimson foil. These are individual gifts for all Loda's male and female relatives, kanzus (long

formal gowns) for the men and gomasis for the women. And then come shoes and wallets and purses, and smaller gifts for the children, until the entire grassy stage looks like a warehouse that has just received several truckloads of new inventory. But it's not over.

A freshly washed white pickup has driven as close as it can get to the guests. In back is a black-and-white cow with a wary look on its face. Two small black goats stand under the cow. Stephen looks at me, and so do all 350 of the guests. "They want you to inspect the cow," he says. My bovine inspection chops are a little rusty, but how can I say no? I walk over to the cow. As I approach, the goats run to the farthest corner of the truck bed. The cow glances at me as if to say, "What now?" And then, under its grassy-smelling breath, it whispers, "I have a bad feeling about this." The goats, too, seem jittery. I turn to the crowd, give a thumbs-up sign, and return to my seat. Stephen hands me a microphone. "They want you to say something."

"Thank you for including me in this great day," I say into the mic. The DJ turns up the volume. "I'm honored to be here." It's so loud the speakers are feeding back into the mic and I sound like Jimi Hendrix at Woodstock, but not in a good way. People grimace and hold their hands to their ears as I finish, "Congratulations to Ben and Loda!" And I was going to add, "And don't take the brown acid," but some remarks just don't translate across cultures. So I didn't.

More is said, and shouted and sung. The crew capturing it all on video slips and slides and zooms and, well, it must have been a chore to edit. The rain and wind descend and toss the tents around a little, and one tent nearly collapses after a small lake forms on top of it, but then, because it's Uganda and because it's a special day for Ben and Loda, the sun suddenly appears and the rain and wind move on to cause havoc elsewhere. The cow and two goats seem to relax.

As the formal part of the ceremony ends, I'm asked to come inside the small living room of Robert's house. Stephen, Livingston, Robert, James and I all take seats against one wall. Ben and several of his brothers sit opposite us. A shallow basket filled with roasted coffee beans is passed around. We all take a few and eat them like peanuts. This is the moment when Ben is accepted as part of the family. Robert's house, and by extension any home that belongs to any member of Loda's family, is now his home as well. Robert says a few words in Luganda about each of his brothers and speaks longest about Loda's late father. Then he turns to me and in English says, "This one is my brother too, but he is a different color because he was born in a different country." We stand, there are handshakes all around the room, and we walk outside to where the food is being served.

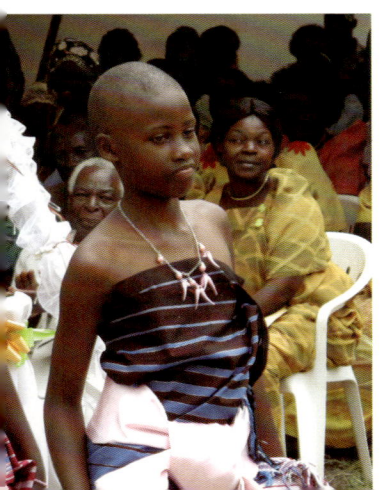

1 DECEMBER 2009

Spellbound on the Mountain

Once again, with Moses the Intrepid as our pilot, somehow we make it – three crushed together in front, five mashed into the back – up, down and over a maze of disintegrating dirt roads cantilevered off lushly upholstered slopes so severe that the banana trees hang on out of sheer terror. And all that needs to be done to harvest the coffee beans is for the villagers to stand shoulder to shoulder on the valley floor on a windy day holding baskets and wait for the ripe red caffeine nuggets to plummet the thousands of feet to earth. The children tie themselves to banana trees and wave at the beans as they glide by.

The question that haunts me during these expeditions is: Which will come first, the end of the road or the end of my rope? Will we arrive before I have a heart attack or am I taking a beat-to-hell Toyota up a Ugandan mountainside to eternity? (It is, by the way, a Windows 7 Toyota: Seven cracks in the windshield. The effect is dazzling. It's like driving while looking through a kaleidoscope.)

We do finally arrive at the end of the road, which, given Moses' skill and driving philosophy, is a good distance after the road ends. Anyway, the car stops, we pop the doors, explode out of the vehicle, and take the first deep breaths we've had for an hour or two. But where are we?

There is not a building in sight. Not even a tree with a bench or a goat skin underneath it. If you look very closely, however, and use the narrowest, sloppiest, most overgrown definition of "trail," there is a "trail." A few thousand feet up it is our destination, a church, built as close to heaven as it can be without having to supply dropdown oxygen masks to the parishioners. Fortunately we have God on our side and it's only moderately sweltering today, mainly because it's about to rain. And as my Africa guru Richard Dowden says, "Nobody ever minds getting wet in Uganda."

For 40 minutes or so, we hike and sweat our way through banana and coffee orchards, potato patches and cassava fields. A very old man leading a very muddy pig on a long braided rope steps aside to let us pass and says "Wasibere" to each one of us. The pig, on the other hand, could not be less interested in our group; she has found a rotting mango in the grass. Occasionally we walk past a hut with the obligatory goat tied to a tree by its front foot and a naked baby or two playing near the door. One toddler, a girl in a green satin dress, smiles at me. I go over to her and extend my hand. She runs away in terror. A little boy, his face covered in cassava flour, musters the courage to approach me. He lets me shake his tiny paw, then reaches up and strokes the hair on my arm. (Most Ugandans don't have much hair on their arms, so the light fur on mine, and the tuft of gray that pokes out above the top button of my shirt, are fascinating to children.)

The church is a 30-by-60-foot mud brick structure with a corrugated metal roof. Inside are several dozen women in brilliantly colored Sunday apparel. It's like diving into a pool of tropical fish. I sit on a bench near a window that looks out at the valley below and beyond that a steep, terraced slope like the one we just climbed. It's a glorious view. Across the chapel, six windows open to a trail that ascends the hill this little church has been built into.

We sit, say little. It's quiet and cool. A few raindrops hit the metal roof. There are some murmurs, children giggle, then out of the near silence comes an exquisite sound. A heavenly human voice -- high and clear, like a sustained note played on a French horn made of porcelain -- overtakes the noise of the rain. The woman singing in the curvaceous sounds of Lhukonzo is to my left, across the aisle. She sings by herself for a couple of minutes, then another woman joins her, and another, and more. Then the children, seated at the side on their own benches, join their mothers and grandmothers, aunts and grown sisters. A handful of men join in too. The singing searches for a moment then blends, merges, finds its own balance, moves. It is one of the most beautiful sounds I've ever heard. So I close my eyes and let it fly me out through the window and over that verdant tropical valley.

Actually, no. My brain doesn't work like that. Instead of flying, I'm fretting. I'm obsessing, preoccupied with what's not rather than what is. Exactly what, I'm wondering, was I thinking when I decided not to bring my unobtrusive, inexpensive, small, light, but surprisingly good-quality digital recorder that will record up to 133 hours. Not a measly 132, mind you, 133! Damn. Eventually, I grow tired of scolding myself over that poor decision, I calm down and listen to the swaying and swimming of voices. If something can be both serene and exhilarating, it is.

The service is about 80 percent singing and 20 percent preaching. A good enough ratio, though 100 percent singing would suit me fine.

I'm a devoted sinner and no amount of hectoring, badgering, terrorizing or belittling is going to change my mind at this late date. I know where I'm headed. I think I'll see a lot of my friends there. (As Twain once said so comfortingly, "Heaven for the climate. Hell for the company.")

As the hypnotic voices mix with the rain and breeze, I cannot take my eyes off of the six windows on the wall opposite me. The path the windows look at rises at a steep angle (what doesn't around here?). Someone's head and shoulders appear in the window at far left, next I see their torso as they pass the second window, then their hips and the bunch of green bananas or the upside-down chicken they're carrying, then, finally, at the last window, just their feet as they disappear up the hill. The rectangular openings are movie screens playing six never-ending attractions in real-time, village life as it passes, in brief cinematic bursts.

In one window is a small boy twirling with an umbrella, turning and nearly tumbling, all the while firmly holding the hook of the umbrella's handle with both hands. But as he moves downhill to the next window, there is no umbrella, only the handle. Like me, he's imagining the rest of the device. Four older boys practice their kung-fu moves, an old woman wearing a bright purple gomasi trudges up the incline holding the hand of a very young child who's earnestly gnawing a piece of sugar cane, two girls lie down in the grass and gaze into the church. They spot me, the only white fish in the tropical crowd, point, laugh and wave.

The singing finishes, the rain ends, the wind dies down, the staring girls grow bored and move on, the clouds sail away, the boy tosses the umbrella handle aside. But the movie just keeps flickering past. It never stops. Ever.

3 DECEMBER 2009

The Coherence of Coincidence

Dust, mud, filth, vile vehicles belching soot, miscellaneous dastardly muck (the sources of which will not be specified), and white clothing without a speck on it. How do the Ugandans do it? One of the many mysteries of this place is the large number of people who wear immaculately white shirts, shoes, head coverings, dresses, ankle-length gomasis and kanzus that stay white all day long as their owners navigate puddles and piles and all manner of funk. I noticed this phenomenon in the first few days I was here. I'd gotten used to it, even forgotten my initial amazement, then it came back to me thanks to the strange and strangely helpful connections the brain makes.

Speaking of which, here I am in a small, electricity-free village in the mountains of Western Uganda. Naturally, one of the first things that's been asked of me is to teach video editing. Yes, there's a group of four or five women who shoot video of many of the activities organized by the coffee farmers cooperative I'm working for. They shoot and shoot and shoot, and they've been doing it since long before I arrived. But they've never edited a single minute of what they've shot. I've been asked to help them learn basic editing, as no one here, or anywhere else, is much interested in watching a four-month-long video.

I immediately said yes. Once committed, however, I belatedly gave it some thought. The video group all grew up on the slopes surrounding this village. They've seen little if any TV. Many have never seen a movie. (I've talked with several villagers who are in their mid-to-late 20s who've never been to Kampala, six hours away.) They've had limited access to picture books. Even magazines and newspapers are not commonly available without traveling by car to a much larger town an hour away. They're rarely exposed to advertising beyond packaging. In other words, though the people of this region possess a long, rich tradition of oral storytelling, their knowledge of the visual narrative techniques that we of the media-besotted world have an almost cellular familiarity with are somewhere between minimal and nonexistent. Which brings us back to the white clothing that seems incapable of getting dirty.

Walking home through the village one afternoon, I'm struggling with the problem before me: How the hell am I going to teach the language of pictures without employing all the references I, though not my students, am intimately familiar with? Fortunately, just about then, two women walk by in pristine white gowns. Seeing them reminds me of Alec Guinness, of course, which in turn reminds me of his 1951 film "The Man in the White Suit," about a miracle fabric that will not get dirty, which in turn makes me think of its director, Alexander Mackendrick, who, after he retired from the movie business, became the dean of the film school at the California Institute of the Arts where, more than 30 years ago, I was his teaching assistant for a class called "Film Grammar."

Sandy, as everyone knew him, was brilliant, to put it mildly, and part of his genius as a teacher was his ability to deconstruct films piece-by-piece and show his students how and why they worked dramatically. He could take apart a movie scene like a science teacher dissecting a frog. But his true greatness and charm came through in the steady stream of anecdotes and digressions that flowed out of him as he illustrated for us the grammatical superstructure of film narrative.

He was on a first-name basis with everyone on the planet, so when he told a story it had a million-dollar cast. He'd once rented his house to Orson Welles who turned out to be the worst tenant of all time and trashed the place. In one class, Sandy demonstrated how you imagine that a wire attached to the top of your head and running through the center of your body is bolted to the floor so that when Burt Lancaster vaults a couch and runs toward you, furious and with fists clenched, you can stand your ground, which is exactly what Sandy managed to do when he was directing Lancaster and Tony Curtis in his noir masterpiece, "The Sweet Smell of Success." For the three years I was around him, Sandy never ran out of stories about Alec Guinness, or scathing remarks about Darryl F. Zanuck with whom he'd had a run-in that proved fatal to his directing career.

As his teaching assistant, I had the extreme good fortune to spend most of one summer helping Sandy prepare for the coming year's classes. He'd decided that the next subjects of his intellectual scalpel would be Bergman's "The Magician" and Hitchcock's "North by Northwest." (Sandy called him "Hitch." Once, when we were screening "Strangers on a Train," he had Hitchcock's daughter, who plays the teenage sister in the film, join us.) What this entailed on my part was spending every day for a few weeks going through both movies virtually frame-by-frame on a Steenbeck film-editing machine with Sandy at my side showing me shot-by-shot how Bergman and Hitchcock achieved their meticulous dramatic constructions. As we went through the films, I made note of the frames Sandy wanted me to take slides of, which he'd use in a lecture for the Film Grammar class. To say it was an excellent education in the internal mechanics and aesthetic nuances of visual storytelling would be an understatement. It was that, to be sure, but it was also one of the great learning experiences of my life. And it was a hell of a good time hanging out in that dark editing room during a hot L.A. summer while being treated to dozens more Sandy stories, such as how, as a British army officer in 1944, he'd helped get movie film in and out of Rome to enable Roberto Rossellini to shoot "Open City" just months after the Allies had driven out the Germans.

I'll never match Sandy's eloquence and his mastery of the subject, but if I can get across just a few of the basics of the visual grammar he explained so well, if I can convey 5 percent of what I learned from him that cinematic summer, I may be able to help the video group here in the Mountains of the Moon to tell their stories in the electronic language of pictures. If so, maybe they can teach me how to keep my white shirt clean for more than 10 minutes after I leave the house.

4 DECEMBER 2009

No One Stops the Rain

The character of the rain here is so distinct — its sweet, musky smell, its equatorial temperature, its enthusiasm, and the extreme effort it makes to get from the clouds to the ground with as much speed and force as possible. I almost wrote fury, but there's no fury in this rain, just insistence; it knows it will go where it's going with no stops along the way. It's torrid, extravagant, Rubenesque rain, not the trim, skittish, jogs-regularly, tentative, whippet rain that comes from drier climates, stingier clouds. And its coffee berry-size drops have bent the landscape, foliage and structures to its will, to let it pass as quickly and efficiently as possible. The Ugandan rain wants to get down from the sky and into the ground, the streams and the rivers right now. It wants to wash all the leaves and slopes, rinse the rocks and trunks, and get sucked up by the subterranean lacework of roots. It will finish here and move on quickly. It has places to go. No time to sightsee, to fritter, to dilly-dally. These are wham bam, thank you, ma'am downpours. This is not weather with a slow hand, no storms here with an easy touch. It's precipitation that comes and goes in a heated rush. Except when it doesn't, when it moves in like low-blowing smoke, tule fog with a payload, swaddles the trees in vapor, lingers above the houses and fields like a misty armada of diaphanous zeppelins unpacking a drenching cargo for an hour or two or three. But those times are rare and when they come you simply stay indoors or hope you can find a very large, sturdy banana leaf. Unless you want to get really, really wet, in which case this is the most cooperative, compliant, agreeable rain you'll ever meet.

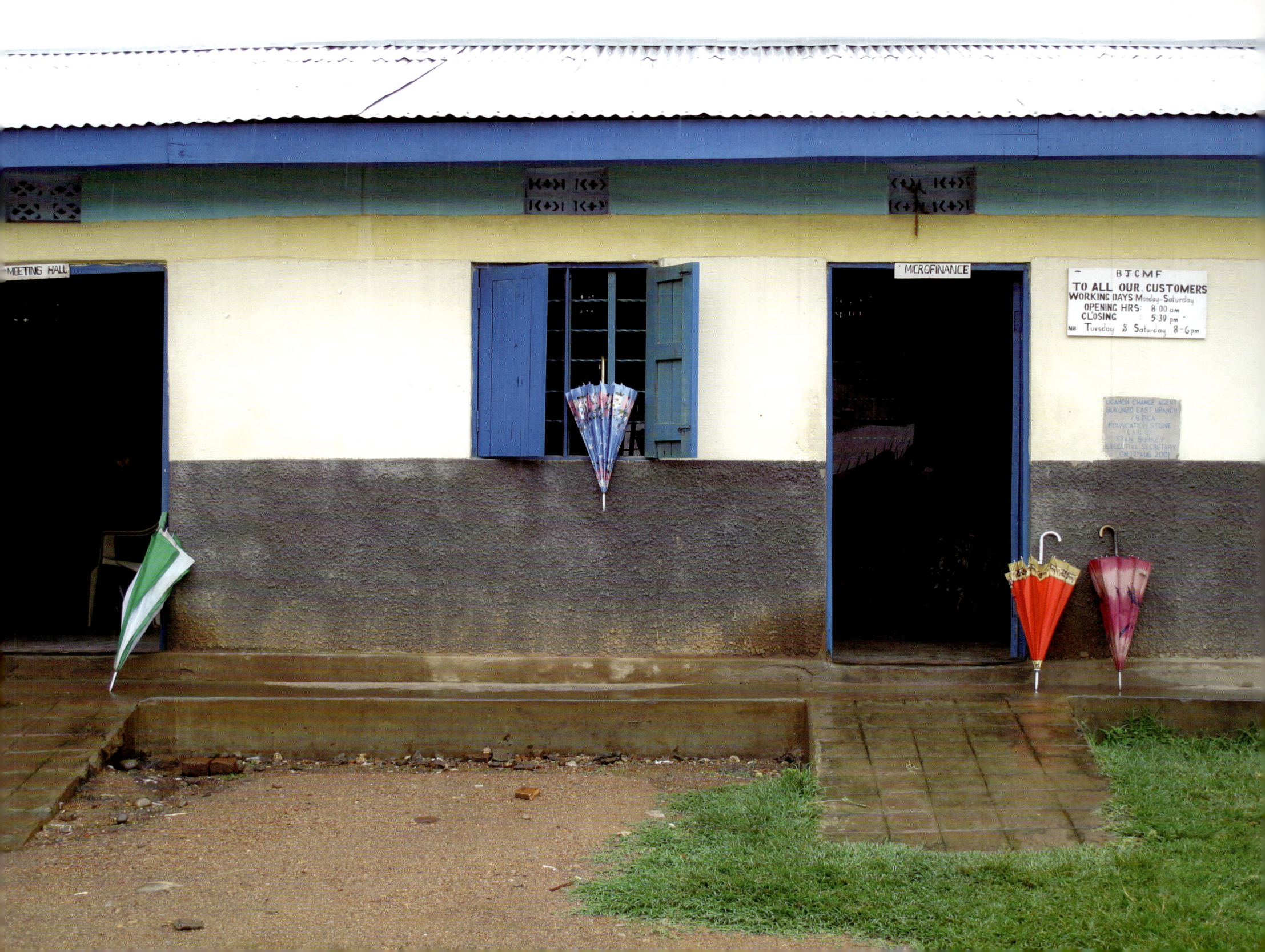

5 DECEMBER 2009

Slow Fade

On nights when I stay in the big town an hour from here, I put up at the White House Hotel. It's small, a dozen or so rooms, and built around a courtyard that often has laundry hanging here and there. Invariably, someone is scrubbing the white tile surfaces, dusting the plants in the lobby. The best rooms have ceiling fans, white mosquito nets draped above the beds, hot showers, toilets and mostly dependable electricity. With a few superficial changes it could just as well be in New Orleans. A double is 30,000 Uganda shillings including breakfast (about $15). It's set far back from the road with a big flat dirt area in front that serves as a stage for the circus-of-life interplay of bicycles, cars, people and boda-bodas that commences before sunrise and continues late into the night. There's a front patio, part of which is covered with a wisteria arbor. In the evenings the staff puts out three or four tables and people congregate, drink lager, order food.

On the second floor, outside the small bar-cafe, is a narrow balcony you can sit on and watch the ever-changing street theater or the sun falling behind the considerably quieter, motionless (though not emotionless) Rwenzori Mountains. The bottles of Eagle, Tusker and Nile Lager at the White House Hotel are always cold, the chips and beef with tomato salad is always comforting, and the echo chamber that is Sky News on the big-screen TV perched over the dining area can always be counted on to deliver the latest catastrophe, calamity or celebrity indiscretion with breathless specificity and an abiding love for the lurid.

Plenty of Ugandan business types stay at the White House, as do backpackers and foreign aid workers — there's usually a U.N., UNICEF, CARE or Save the Children SUV parked out front. And if luck is with me there's one or more of my favorite fellow guests: the out-of-round, iconoclastic expat. Sometimes they're British, other times Dutch, German or French, occasionally American.

Recently when I was there, I was sitting out on the balcony with an Eagle Lager for company when a large Englishman with shaggy gray hair, dressed in shorts and a T-shirt that was a size too small for him, walked out and took a chair nearby. We chatted about nothing in particular for awhile as we worked our way down to conversational bedrock. Ian Patrick Teale was his name. I remember because he repeated the entire thing twice when I asked him. He'd started traveling here on business from his home on the fringes of London when the big copper mine was still in operation up at Kilembe, made friends, loved the country, finally decided to make it his home.

"Get back to London much?"

"Every year or two, but I see fewer friends every time. I've been living here 16 years now. Friends back home slowly fade away. After you get used to this place, one doesn't visit England for the weather. And when you do return, or even make a call over there, there's less and less to talk about. The common points of reference diminish rather quickly. My everyday life, just walking down the road, is so radically different than anything anyone I know in London experiences that I might as well have moved to another planet."

"Yeah," I said, "I can see how that would be."

"People who haven't been here don't know what to make of Africa. They can't imagine. They only know what they see on that," Ian said, as he pointed with his thumb behind our backs to the TV partly visible through the window.

"Tragedy porn," I said.

He laughed so hard he started coughing. "There you go, mate. Righto, they think that sums up the place."

"It doesn't," I said.

"No," he said. "It doesn't. Not nearly. Not even close." He took a final gulp of his Tusker, smiled and nodded. "Good night, mate," he said and went inside.

7 DECEMBER 2009

You Still Working on That?

What's up with predators? They act so damn, I dunno, predatory. Facing the unsettling beasts with nothing between you and them but the not entirely comforting fact that you're precariously seated on the roof of a bucking Land Rover sobers you right up. Their power drill gaze makes an inarguable assertion: "I'm bad. Don't mess with me. I will eat you." And if you're into push-back, they're ready: "Don't try to out-stare me: I can look directly into your eyes without blinking for the next several hours, days or months."

The elephants are different. They aren't technically predators unless you're a maize farmer, in which case they're definitely predators. But as vegetarians they take a more benign approach than the straight-up badasses of the veldt. If you're invading their space, elephants have a combination glance, snort, ear flap thing they do that says, "Do you want to be sent home in a manila envelope? No? Then you have four seconds to back off. Make that none seconds … Done and done and Bob's your uncle. Somebody hand me a spatula. Yes, yes, I get that all the time: It is amazing how fast four tons can move."

Hippos take a similar approach, except for the benign part and the warning signs, and at a wrenlike three tons, they're lighter on their feet than elephants. They simply appear out of nowhere, trample you, then go back to their reading. (In the hippo department, here's a fun game: Once you let it be known that you're going to Africa, keep a count of how many times you're told, "Hippos kill more people than lions." When it comes to animal-related bromides, I believe you'll find it beats "My dog thinks it's a person" and "My dog is part wolf" 3-to-1.)

As for lions, are they cool or are they cool? They're ice, they're dry ice, they're Ice 9! They're cooler than Keith Richards and Miles Davis combined, and throw Angelique Kidjo into the mix. And lions invented the pimp roll. Male or female, they walk with that workin'-my-shoulders-like-I'm-boxin'-in-a-big-vat-of-honey air of self-possession.

Hanging on to the roof rack of the Rover, so as not to get bounced off and become somebody's brunch, my attention zooms into three lion gals strolling in a row in the tall grass, parallel to the road and maybe 150 yards away. They're returning from breakfast, oozing glacial confidence. "Yes," they seem to be thinking, "we are pretty damned pleased with ourselves. Wouldn't you be? Check it out: We've got it all, wrapped in a hot, sleek package. We're built for style, comfort and speed. This thing moves and then stops on a dime, takes care o' business. We can drop a waterbuck or a cape buffalo, gnosh to our hearts' content, and be back posing for tourists and doing the lick-licknuzzle mommy thing with the cubs before the morning sun lights up the euphorbia candelabra. Female empowerment? Around here we spell it L-I-O-N-E-S-S."

Even the hyenas, the intellectuals of the savannah, are impressed by the lions. Not intimidated necessarily. Let's just say there's a degree of professional respect, an acknowledgment of expertise. If you read up on hyenas, you'll find that the phrase "bone-crushing jaws" occurs in the literature with unpleasant frequency. A hard to hide glee on the parts of the authors is tucked between the lines. But they can be forgiven. There's a lot of downtime when you're doing field research in Africa. You're working, but you're also waiting. And while you're waiting, you're ruminating, and maybe sketching out your thesis or revising a peer-reviewed scientific paper that's filled with dismal graphs on stool sample analysis. The temptation to liven things up with a phrase like "bone-crushing jaws" is apparently irresistible.

In any case, hyenas are strange and anomalous creatures, in terms of their looks, their behavior and their anatomy. Many people assume they're a type of wild dog, but they veered away from canines quite a few offramps back on the evolutionary turnpike. They're more closely related to meerkats. Hyenas are highly intelligent, hunt in tight, complex collaboration, and they're flexible. If the hunting is slow, no worries, they'll scavenge, which was what the one I came across seemed to be doing. (I'm told it's rare to see one alone.) The waterbuck carcass he was snacking on had probably been left behind by the lionesses, who assigned him cleanup duty before they departed. There wasn't much left but the horns, the lower legs and the rib cage, which is why it's so handy to have bone-crushing jaws.

13 DECEMBER 2009

Don't It Make My Blue Mind Blown

Shortly after yesterday's tyrannosaurusly torrential rainathon, more of us than I could count piled into what Moses the Intrepid calls the Muzungu Mobile, featuring Muzungu Four Wheel Drive: If we get stuck, I get out and push. Fortunately, because Moses is the best driver in Uganda, we've never gotten stuck, so the Muzungu Four Wheel Drive feature had yet to be called into service — until yesterday, when things unraveled like so:

Late afternoon, and it's still soggy outside as we fill every corner of the Toyota and hang whatever we can out the windows (as usual, I'm the only muzungu in the Muzungu Mobile). We slip and slither down what was a road before the cloud blast and is now a deeply rutted, extremely mushy riverbed, generously sprinkled with branches and boulders and old flip-flops and anything else that tends to head downhill when vast quantities of water are racing for the valleys. It's like driving down a boulevard of Jello — Jello with fruit chunks in it.

Usually on these rides, as the Lhukonzo is fired back and forth at an impossible to follow velocity, I just watch the sights while roving around the more remote regions of my own personal planet. In this case, I get to wondering about Crystal Gayle and her ankle-length hair and what she's been up to since her luscious, cowboy-jazzy late '70s hit "Don't It Make My Brown Eyes Blue." Country music from that period is in heavy rotation on the local radio stations, and tunes from those years keep popping into my consciousness unexpectedly. But even if Crystal were up ahead with her thumb stuck out, there would be nowhere to put her, except on the roof, her 4-foot-long tresses streaming behind us, a testament to the structural integrity of keratin and the utility of anti-tangle conditioner. Then I'm reminded of Isadora Duncan's horrific fate and the weird fact that the scarf that did her in was loaned to her by Preston Sturges' mother just before the car pulled away, and then, because of the "brown eyes blue" refrain of the song, I think of blue-headed agamas, Ugandan lizards that unquestionably deserve a place in the pantheon of mind-blowing beasties and which I've written about before.

After maybe 90 seconds of such mental dithering, I exhaust my knowledge of Crystal Gayle, Isadora Duncan and African reptiles and find myself stalled in a daydream cul-de-sac. Moments later I'm liberated from it when we pass a new sedan carrying not one but two pastors with a civilian driver at the wheel. Moses pulls over and gets out of the Muzungu Mobile. I follow him. The two pastors and their driver are seriously bogged down in the muck, but the driver continues to spin the wheels in the slippery stuff.

"Tell him to stop that," I say to Moses. "Reverse is the lowest gear. They gotta go back, not try to go forward." Moses convinces the driver to let him give it a try. The guy gets out, Moses gets in. I walk to the passenger side, put my weight against the front fender and, for the first time since arriving here, implement Muzungu Four Wheel Drive. I do little to help, though I do grunt and stumble dramatically. Moses, on the other hand, very, very gently and skillfully coaxes the vehicle out of the swamp, then pulls it around the dirt pudding and ahead to where the road is comparatively firm and dry. There is a brief roadside concert of back slapping, thanking and hand shaking. One of the pastors says, "God bless you both," and then we depart, content in the knowledge that we have marginally increased our chances of getting into heaven.

Not far from the Kisinga roundabout at the bottom of the grade, we stop and wait while some Ankole cattle carry their humongous horns across the road (a second, even more dramatic testament to the structural integrity of keratin). We're about 3 feet from a rain-dampened wall. The sun is hitting it, pulling vapor out of the mud bricks. Moses is fiddling with the radio, an ongoing occupation of his. I glance over at the wall. Staring back at me, almost within grabbing distance, is a blue-headed agama. I lean a little closer. His tongue darts in and out, but he doesn't flinch. Without taking my eyes off of him, I search my shoulder bag for my camera. I find it and slowly raise it to my eyes. This agama has nerves of keratin. He turns his head to offer his profile. What a handsome little Lucifer he is, a regular John Barrymore — with scales. Click, click, click. He even lets me take a few more, then he's done and gone. Crystal Gayle, however, whom Moses has found on the radio, is just beginning: "Don't know when I've been so blue ..."

16 DECEMBER 2009

Landscaping the Mountains of the Moon

The initial impression when coming up the long dirt road that splits off from the paved route to the Congo and winds past banana groves and coffee orchards before arriving at the village I live in is of going into deep country. If not complete wildness, then a reasonable facsimile. The first views while ascending out of the thorn tree savannah and the maize fields are of lush, overgrown slopes that rise to forested foothills that reach up to clouds swaddling ragged, not-very-distant peaks, one of which, Mount Margherita, exceeds 16,000 feet and, like several of its siblings, is rarely visible. Below, separating the village's east and west sides, is a rambunctious, somersaulting river filled with pachyderm-size boulders that shambles and spills and splashes out of the Rwenzoris, the Mountains of the Moon that border the Great Rift Valley on its western edge, and which are the dividing line between Uganda and the Democratic Republic of Congo, an optimistic misnomer if there ever was one.

Before you've focused, before you've stared at and studied the terrain and the flora, you think "wild." But it's the opposite. People and lots of them have lived around here for centuries and centuries, and the land has been entirely transformed. The impossibly steep hillsides that were once carpeted with trees resemble the checker-field farm country of Iowa or Indiana turned on a severe diagonal. These high hills have been farmed and manicured and cultivated since God was a toddler. This place has been lived on and cared for and carved by humans longer than England's hunt country, France's Loire Valley, or Tuscany, and sometimes if the light's right, if you squint and look in just the right direction for only a moment, it can resemble all of them.

To the unacquainted eye the fields appear chaotic, but as you start to really see it all, and walk through it, it's clear that it's been precisely landscaped, with borders and pathways and homes and hedgerows and miniature reservoirs. The farms and terracing extend upward to an extraordinary height, but beyond a certain altitude thick tree cover still carpets the land. (One local insisted to me that mountain gorillas continue to live in that mist-shrouded tangle, half a day's hike from this village. I think he's mistaken, but not by much. If you kept trekking for another day you'd cross into Congo's Virunga Mountains, one of the last outposts of the baddest vegetarians on the planet.) Finally, most large foliage gives up the battle as cliffs, rocks, a few preternaturally hardy mammoth succulents, peat bogs, marshy deltas, montane grasslands, snowfields and rapidly shrinking glaciers take over.

18 DECEMBER 2009

True Fabrications

Walking down the road here one comes across visual delicacies daily, hourly and minute by minute. One of the tastiest is the boldly patterned cotton fabric that men, women and children wrap themselves in. It comes in endless variations and is everywhere in the open air markets, the shops, flying from clotheslines like campaign banners for the Hallucination Party and draped over bushes to dry.

It broadcasts amplified colors and shapes that reference all sorts of graphical and artistic influences, but it is unmistakably and irrevocably African, and its origins thread through a visual tradition that goes back centuries, if not tens of centuries.

At first, I thought I'd seen something like it, but after a longer look I realized, no, most of it is utterly unique; I've never seen anything truly similar. Brazenly original in conception and execution, it can be startling and jolting, but also exceptionally subtle and nuanced in its design and the fearless use of color.

My schooling in composition came from spending many an evening as a vision-hungry adolescent poring over large books of the magnificent polychrome woodcuts from Japan's Ukiyo-e (Floating World) period by artists such as Utamaru, Moronobu, Kiyonobu, Kiyonaga, Harunobu, Kunichika, Hiroshige, Sharaku and Hokusai. Somewhere, when I was 13 or 14, I also got my hands on a book of Japanese crests and spent weeks studying those.

Whatever I learned of visual balance, graphic design and the secret language of shape, line, color and juxtaposition started during those elevated nights staring into volumes of intoxicating, gorgeously crafted images. The anonymous crest creators and the Floating World artists left an indelible impression, and looking at this African fabric every day has brought that back.

Not that the fabric designs here resemble the Japanese work, though occasionally there is an echo. The one reminding me of the other has more to do with emotional memory: As with those teenage vision feasts decades ago, something is stirred, thrilled and mildly stoned by the assertiveness of the graphical imagination that invented such strange, powerful, perfect imagery.

27 DECEMBER 2009

Drama King of the Beasts

You get a crowd of baboons together on a winter's day and it starts to feel a lot like Christmas. There's no explaining it, it's one of those seasonal inevitabilities. You need several of the personable primates, at least. A dozen and a half is ideal. The other day, blessed with good fortune, I found myself sharing tidings of comfort and joy with 20 or so of our distant relatives.

A friend and I were on a meandering stroll under a gray Christmas Day sky when down the road a boy motioned to us and pointed into the brush. We went to where he was standing and looked. About 40 feet away in a clearing was a large troop of the dog-nosed monkeys doing all the things that animals do. Some of those things are done only in private by most Homo sapiens, but baboons have no such hang-ups (or laws or cellphone cameras or salacious websites or lawyers or prenups) and, to paraphrase the Beatles, they have no compunction about doing it in the road. Given that it was Christmas, we'd already opened our presents and we're curious souls, we watched the floor show. Besides, my friend was intent on getting photographic documentation of the alpha male in flagrante delicto with the alpha mama (for educational purposes, of course, but also to decorate a Facebook page).

Holidays get everyone worked into a fever pitch of angst, elation, depression, lust, enervation, forced camaraderie, alienation, manic weirdness, phony good cheer, authentic good cheer and not-always-pleasant family dynamics -- the whole delicious cornucopia of emotions, only amplified. Baboons are no exception. Observing the troop for nearly an hour, we were treated to a non-hominid opera, the best and worst of baboon behaviors: Love, insecurity, warmth, aloofness, domestic violence and strange acting out were all on display, sometimes simultaneously. The sexual high jinks were the least of it.

Things began to come unglued just as the second or third (very brief) amorous coupling was winding down, and one of the younger up-and-coming males remembered the monkey-see, monkey-do concept and thought, "I'm in the mood for love." The alpha male took violent exception to that bright idea, shrieked, ran toward the young gun, bared his scary-looking fangs, and chased the randy upstart into a tree where he stayed, sulking bitterly, for the balance of our visit. That event put a distinct damper on further amore, but tenderness ensued in the afterglow as the entire family took to gently, meticulously grooming one another. I craved a cigarette.

Everything seemed to be getting back to hunky-dory when alpha mama decided she'd had about enough of the baby hanging beneath her nursing. She knocked the insistent little sucker to the ground, which evoked an ear-splitting howl that easily exceeded the vocal gymnastics of both Yma Sumac and Howard Dean. The loudly protesting -- unhurt, but unhappy -- baby ran over to the alpha male who held the youngster against his stomach, tenderly stroking it until it quieted down. At that point, a female with an older baby came over and tried to make time with the alpha male. The cranky nursing mother, alpha mama, was having none of that, so she whacked the flirtatious tart's offspring, causing the innocent tyke and its trampy mother to flee. The alpha male, who clearly knew when to hold 'em and when to fold 'em, quickly sought some solitude by turning his back on the drama and becoming fascinated with his leg. He stared at his own knee for about five minutes. I think it's called transference.

Whatever it's called, it was very effective, a psychological masterstroke. Soon alpha mama was tidying up his back, her baby was contentedly nursing, and the spirit of Christmas once again warmed the rain forest.

1 JANUARY 2010

Born Again

Some prefer the cake of being born again without the frosting of religion slathered on it. New Year's is that, after a fashion: It offers a dramatic transition, the ritual welcoming of the future, washing away the past, at least what can be washed away. But there are also those things — people, experiences, abilities, love — that slip into the past whether we want them to or not.

About 9:30 New Year's Eve I got a text message from a friend, Josephine, who lives near Kampala. She's the matriarch of a terrific family that I stayed with the first 10 weeks I was here. After bringing up five sons and a daughter, Josephine is now raising five of her grandchildren. She wished me a good 2010 and happily informed me that her daughter-in-law, Linda, had given birth to her first child, a girl. I always liked Linda. She's with Josephine's reggae-loving son Isaac, a law student, a very savvy guy and a kind soul. Linda used to talk to me about her father, who lives in Seattle, and about how much she wanted to go to the USA.

"What's the first thing you'll do when you get there?" I asked her once.

"I'll find the tallest building," she said, "and go to the top of it."

"And?" I asked.

"Just look and look and look."

Early New Year's day morning I heard from another friend who, the night before, was told by a girl he had fallen in love with that she no longer wanted him to be part of her life, didn't want to hear from him, didn't want to see him. This young guy used to tell me in rhapsodic terms how enchanted he was with her, how perfect she was for him, how funny she was. Why do people do things like that on New Year's?

"That was last year," I said unhelpfully. (I never know the appropriate thing to say or do at such times, and I can assure you, having been through them myself, no one else does either.) "This is next year. Onward." Then I told him something from which he seemed to derive slightly more solace. My mother said it to me more than 40 years ago when I was a freshly heartbroken teenager and wanted to die. "Nothing is as permanent as a first love," she told me that late August afternoon, "except the impermanence of the second and third."

It didn't cheer me any more than it cheered my friend 40 years later.

What it did for me was help me zoom out a little, move the magnifying glass away from my eye and take in the whole view, just for a moment, so I could return to my suffering with a small glimmer of light visible on the horizon of my life. Maybe it did the same for him. Maybe not.

Later in the morning, walking to work, making my way past baby pigs and elderly drunks, somebody behind me yelled my name. I turned to see Augustine 40 or 50 feet down the road, his cap pulled down low over his eyes. When our driver, Moses, gets busy he brings in Augustine to handle the overflow. Augustine is not as entertaining as Moses, and we don't joke and banter as much as Moses and I do, but he's a warm, solid character, a careful driver, and we always stop and talk when we meet in town. I'd run into Augustine on my way home New Year's Eve and he'd been especially buoyant, looking forward to going out with friends. Early on the first day of the year he didn't look like he was coming off a night of partying.

He walked up to me. I shook his hand. "Happy New Year."

"Yes," he said. "But it starts with a problem."

"What problem?"

"My father died last night." He was in that state of grief-stricken disbelief that you inhabit in the first hours after hearing that someone close to you has passed away. "We'll put him over there," he said, pointing toward the cemetery on the southeastern edge of town.

I told him I was sorry, stood with him for several long, silent minutes. Then he said he had to go and I headed up to my office. As I walked away from Augustine, I started humming a familiar song, but I couldn't immediately place it. Music from the distant past pops into my head all the time. Occasionally I'll hum and whistle a piece for weeks before I can figure out what it is. This one didn't take that long, perhaps because it's from one of my favorite albums, the Pretenders' "Learning to Crawl." The song is "Thumbelina," a great ballad, a spacious on-the-road song of loss and renewal, in which Chrissie Hynde wraps her voluptuous tenor around lyrics that manage to be desperate and hopeful all at once:

> *Hush little baby, don't you cry*
> *When we get to Tucson you'll see why*
> *We left the snowstorms and the thunder and rain*
> *For the desert sun, we're gonna be born again ...*

4 JANUARY 2010

Department of Synchronicity

It happened again.

I'm lying in bed trying to see through the cerulean blue mosquito net and determine what time the small, dependably inaccurate travel clock across the room thinks it is. It thinks it's 6 A.M. It's wrong. It's 6:30. I know that because Roselin is always out in the courtyard doing her dishes at 6:30.

An easily recognizable song that I don't recognize is going through my head. Another is coming into my ears, a lovely one, being sung by Roselin. Roselin always sings when she's washing her dishes or doing her laundry or bathing or doing most anything. She has a high, beautiful voice that belongs in a '30s or '40s movie musical and she's not shy about using it. She's a young Ugandan Jeanette MacDonald.

Later, she's making breakfast while trilling poignant, round words in Lhukonzo as I'm walking across the courtyard from the shower. "I love your singing, Roselin," I say. She laughs and laughs. I've told her before and she always thinks it's funny.

Around noon, at work, I'm typing away at the computer and Roselin comes in and tells me to save everything. The solar power is about to automatically shut off because it's been cloudy all day. "Make the clouds go away, Roselin. If you'd sing the sun would come out."

"No," she says. "I've been singing all morning and it has not come out." At that moment I recall the song that was going through my head when I first woke to Roselin's singing. It's one I used to play regularly when I did a radio show more than 35 years ago. I'm sure I haven't listened to it in at least three decades. It's the old Robert Hunter-Jerry Garcia tune "Bird Song." The first line is: "All I know is something like a bird within her sang ..."

Just another day in the brain's oddly curving corridors of coincidence.

7 JANUARY 2010

Attack of the Recalcitrant Mooncalves

Being the mother or father of an underperformer is one of parenthood's greatest challenges. You try to set a good example, introduce them to sound judgment and cool, crisp reasoning, guide them, nurture them, reward their successes and help them put their failures behind them. Still, in the dark of night or the glare of the noonday sun, events may conspire to force you to see the truth, no matter how dismaying and disheartening, and admit that your youngster — though he or she may be cute as a bug's ear — is simply not the brightest thing on four legs.

Yesterday such a scene played out right before my eyes. Moses and I were in the Muzungu Mobile mobilizing down to the Congo road at a smart clip with no traffic ahead of or behind us and no other obstacles to impede our rocketlike progress save the occasional hysteria-addled goat struggling to make a decision as to which side of the road to run toward and bolting madly back and forth while prudently weighing its choices.

We were chattering aimlessly in a mix of English and Lhukonzo, happy as clams would be if clams could drive down a wide, flat, nicely groomed dirt lane lined with vast maize fields and watched over by an armada of well-stuffed, freshly laundered clouds. Then we rounded a turn and our intoxicating freedom and levity was abruptly halted by a wide river of Ankole cows moving from one pasture to another while their herder boy leaned against a mango tree talking on his cellphone.

No problem. It was a motivated bunch. Some even broke into a trot, so excited were they by the tall green smorgasbord stretched out before them. Behind the main group, however, in the caboose position, came two calves being pushed forward by two long-suffering cows that had clearly had it up to the tips of their gracefully arcing horns with their sluggish, distracted progeny. The calves had no light in their eyes; they possessed a studied dullness, an incuriousness. They gave the immediate impression that if there was a smart decision to be made neither of them would make it, and they would both defend the other one's misjudgment — to the death if necessary.

Meanwhile, the mothers of these two were obviously thinking, "What wouldn't we give for just a few uninterrupted hours of lounging in the tall grass, bathed by the Ugandan sun, chewing our cud, and staring out at the Great Rift Valley without these two goosebrained ninnies hectoring us incessantly for milk while coming up with one idiotic plan after another?"

At that very moment, as if to make the point for their beleaguered mothers, the two jabbernows decided they'd square off against the Muzungu Mobile, which Moses was ever so slowly and gingerly easing forward, trying to nudge aside the herd so we could resume our flight.

With no provocation, and certainly no encouragement from their moms who were headed straight for the waiting feast, the two bovine peckerwoods transported themselves to Barcelona, Sunday afternoon, 1940 something. They imagined that both Hemingway and Picasso were in the stands. They backed up, they lunged, they went all theatrical, got all up in our grillwork like a couple of drunk and surly sailors on shore leave and spoiling for a fight.

"Should I?" Moses asked. His palm hovered over the horn.

"Educate them," I said.

He gave them a long, loud blast.

Man-o-War and Secretariat never moved so fast. Those calves levitated. They went airborne. They went FedEx. They looked like cow-shaped Harrier jump jets. They were at the table with their bibs on, saying grace, several minutes ahead of the rest of the herd.

Their mothers, on the other hand, didn't even glance in our direction. But I think I did see one of them shake her head a little and sigh.

11 JANUARY 2010

Channeling

The Kazinga Channel in western Uganda is a broad, natural rope of water more than 30 kilometers long. It tethers Lake Edward to Lake George, and it is Hippopalooza every day of the week and twice on Sundays; it hosts one of the most abundant concentrations of the portly, ill-tempered submersibles in all of Africa. Cape buffalo, which are devoted mud wallowers, keep the hippos company and Nile crocodiles provide security, insecurity and all around dramatic tension. There are also elephants, some of the biggest I've seen, and a mind-boggling variety of bird life, including African fish eagles, which look a lot like American bald eagles, white pelicans, and the petulant pouting shoebill (or whale-headed) stork (given the names the poor creature has been saddled with, who could blame it for pouting?).

There are few more pleasant ways to spend a couple of hours than cruising down the Channel, coming as close as prudence allows to the beasts, gawking at them, photographing them, strolling the upper deck to watch the honeymooners necking, and spacing on the ongoing cloud show that resembles something you might witness while flying through the atmosphere of a distant planet.

If you spend your days as an elephant or hippo, hauling around a body that weighs more than an SUV, it must feel exquisite to slip into the water and let natural buoyancy take over for an hour or two or 12. Indeed, most of them and their pups spend much of the day in the Channel, though even hippos have to work on their tans. And when the time comes they don't seem to mind fraternizing with the cape buffalo and the crocodiles, though sometimes things get a tad operatic. At one point, a crocodile on the bank slowly wriggled toward a succulent infant hippo napping next to its mama. The mama twirled her ears, flicked her tail and belched, "Make my day." The croc backpedaled triple fast.

One great-grandfather pachyderm, a gigantic bull, kept himself nearly submerged as we floated by, tracking us with his eyes, rhythmically spraying himself with water from his trunk as the spirit moved him. Once we'd passed, and ruined his reverie, his afternoon's meditation, he wearily pulled himself out of the drink, like a submarine surfacing, gallons and gallons of water running off his massive carcass, and climbed the slope to the grassy bank. Dark gray-blue, he appeared to be made of clay and finished with a high-gloss glaze.

As the sun began to fall, going from yellow to orange to scarlet, with violet-pink mixed in, we headed back to the dock. Far across the Channel, the graceful, low-slung boats were fanning out across the water for night fishing, and the hippos were clambering up on the bank to moon bathe and dream the large, large dreams that only they can dream.

16 JANUARY 2010

No Sun King

It starts with the animals acting slightly strange. The local dog choir does a rare post-dawn performance, the blue-headed agamas freeze in place on the rooftops and branches. The birds, just wiping the sleep from little ebony eyes, hunker down in the trees, confused, thinking that their body clock is on the fritz because it's telling them they need to go back to dreamland, even though that's where they just came from. Then you begin feeling a little strange because the crackling white light of morning is turning to deep orange and getting dimmer by the moment. What up?

Annular solar eclipse, that's what. And not just any old eclipse. Yesterday's magnificent celestial stunt was a brief, but dazzling bit of sun-moon acrobatics, the likes of which we won't see again any time soon and most on the planet never saw at all, except on computer screens and newspaper pages. Around here, people used window reflections or a plastic basin filled with water, or peered through thin napkins to avoid gazing directly at the sun. The best shield, however, was the roiling cloud curtain that would completely obliterate the twinned orbs for a few seconds, then teasingly reveal them through a veil of vapor, which once or twice provided a glare-free projection screen, and cut the light enough to enable photos, such as the one at left, which I took at about 8:15 a.m. in Kasese, Uganda.

"That's a good omen," I said to a Ugandan friend after the show was over and we were heading to breakfast. I just made that up. I didn't know whether it was or not, and besides, I'm not really into omens. Turns out I was right.

About six hours later, the heat of the afternoon having put me in a semi-dream state, the same friend came to my door. "Would you like to go see the king?" she asked. She'd read my mind. Not five minutes before I'd been thinking that I wished I knew a king so I could go visit him. Wish granted! And we didn't even have to go far. His palace is less than a mile from where I'm staying. On occasion you do get what you want. Sometimes this old universe ain't so bad after all.

He is Omusinga Charles Wesley Mumbere Irema-Ngoma of Rwenzururu, the king of the Rwenzori Kingdom. He was reinstated to the throne just last October after an absence of many years, during which he worked as a nurses' aide in the United States. On the spur of the moment, a small group of college students he was scheduled to meet with asked if we'd like to accompany them. My friend said she thought we would and came and got me. And that's the true story of how my wish was granted and we stumbled into an audience with his highness, the Omusinga of Rwenzururu.

We arrived at the palace in the hills behind this town to find several Ugandan army guards at the gate, AK-47s slung over their shoulders. An officer walked over and greeted us, then we were frisked, asked to turn off our cellphones and to turn on our cameras. The officer inspected the cameras and handed them back to us and said we could use them only "on request." He motioned for us to follow him. We walked past a royal guard who was holding a spear. Both his white shirt and his gray cap were embroidered with the phrase "Royal Guard."

The throne room was in a large, low, cylindrical building with a gently sloping, conical roof. The entire structure was made of logs and reeds. It was cool and dark inside; a timid breeze moved through the open hexagonal windows. Unadorned fluorescent tubes attached to the walls in three or four places provided the only artificial light. The dirt floor had been swept clean. There were a few thick ribbons -- yellow and blue -- tied on supporting eaves, some palm fronds lashed to pillars, but the room was largely free of decoration. There were several rows of wooden benches. We sat down. At the front was a raised platform with a desk-size table and a large cushioned chair. The table covering was oddly incongruous. It appeared to be a sheet for a child's bed. Its border featured brightly colored cartoon figures of animals and a wooden ship with a barn on its deck: Noah's Ark.

We waited for 30 or 40 butt-anesthetizing minutes, then a small procession entered led by the king. Two ministers, several officers and three ladies of the court followed him. In his right hand he was carrying a short fly-whisk with a black and white diamond design on the handle. He was dressed in gray slacks and a short-sleeve white shirt. His glasses had thin gold rims. He looked to be in his mid-50s. He took his place at the table on the platform. The army officer who'd inspected our cameras sat behind the king in a white plastic chair.

We prayed and sang the anthem of the Rwenzori kingdom and the Uganda national anthem. We then introduced ourselves individually, after which the president of the student association read a long document. The king listened intently, making notes and nodding. After the reading was complete, the king addressed each issue that had been raised. The minister of education said he'd been a founder of the student association more than 20 years ago. We sang again. We prayed again. The king rose and exited, followed by his ministers, several officers and the three ladies of the court, one of whom carried his empty water glass in a small black suitcase.

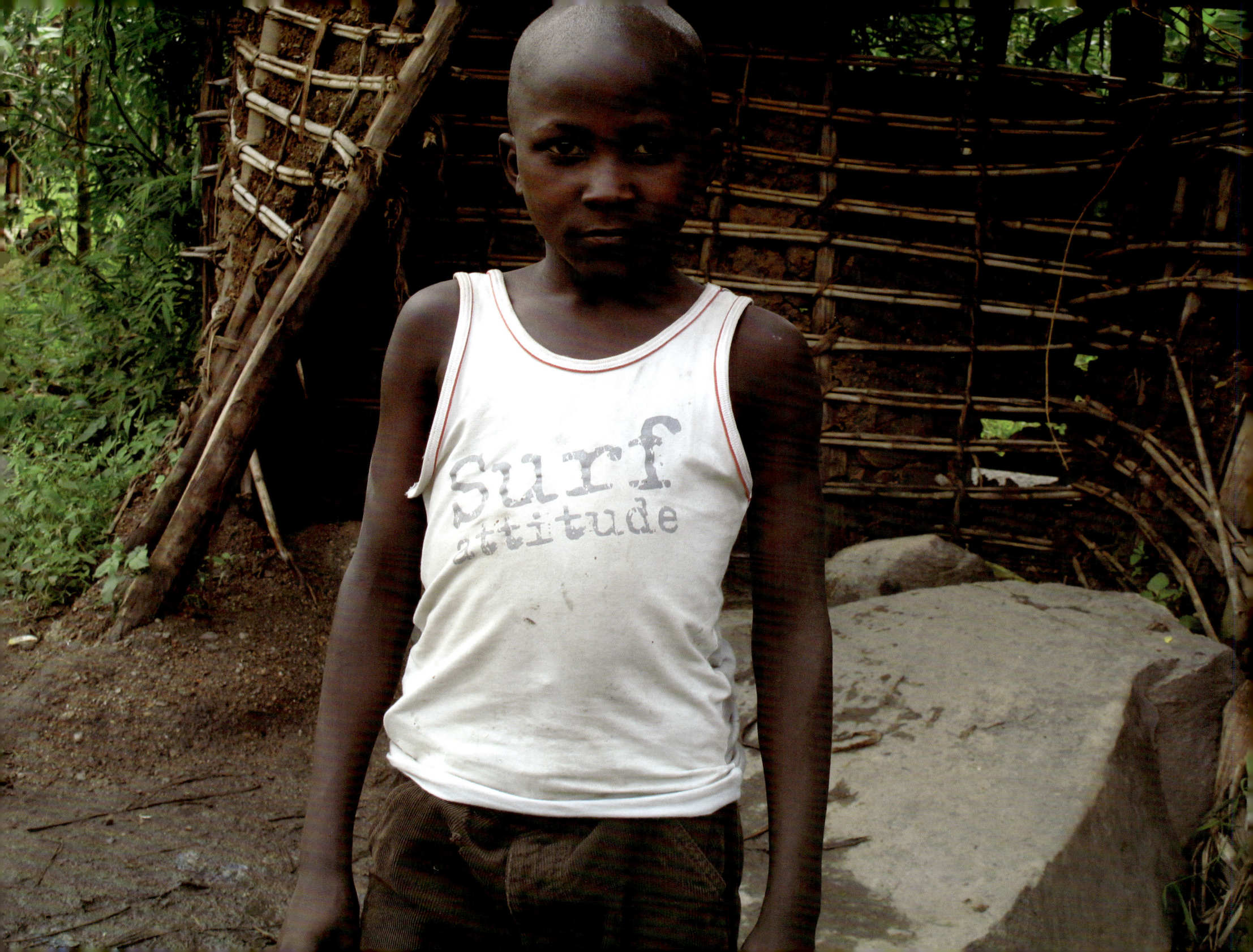

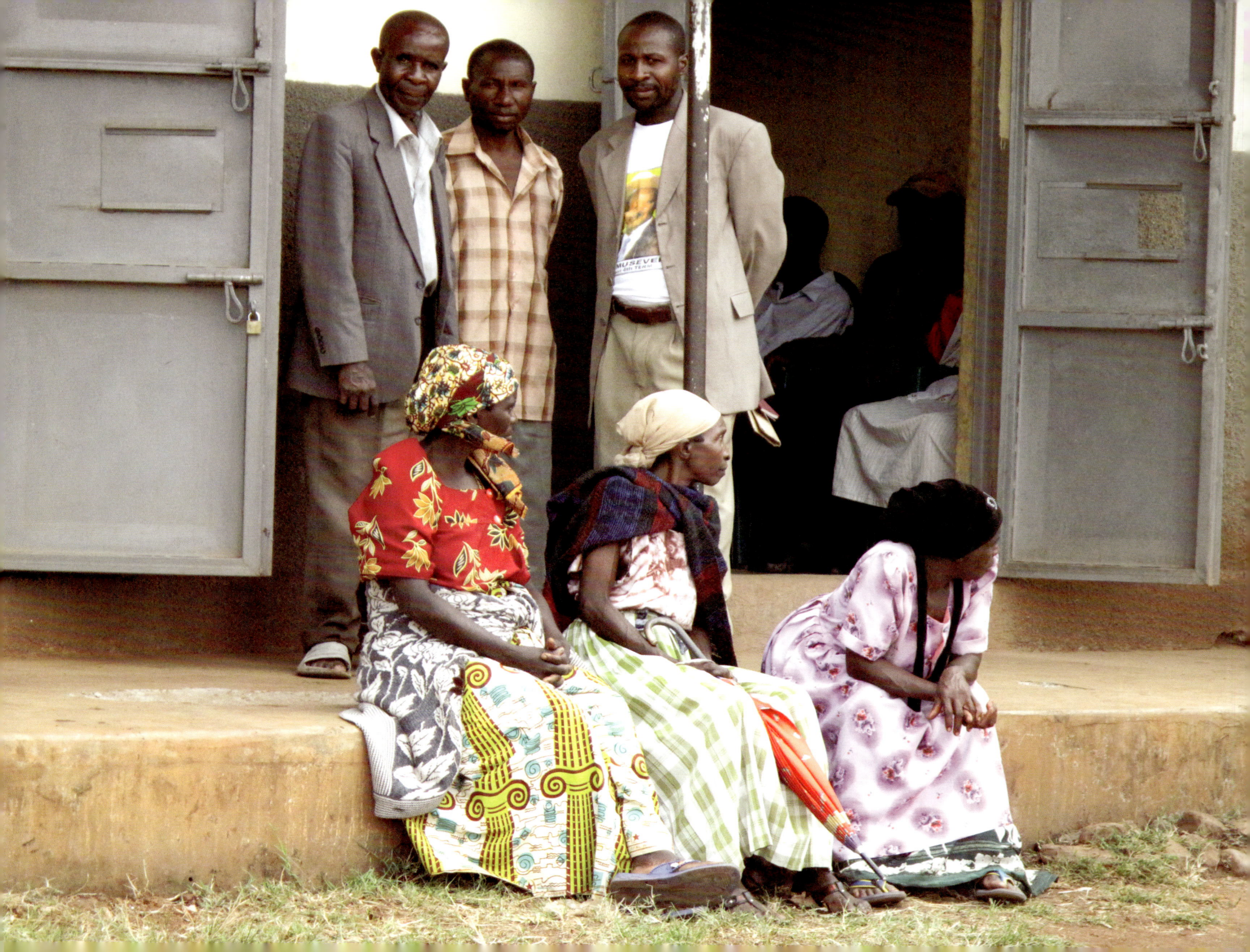

25 JANUARY 2010

A Permit to Visit the Relatives

It's amazing what you can accomplish when you show up with a big bag of money. Politicians and their patrons have known that for years, but I'm an innocent little flower and though I recently turned 57, I'm just catching on to the ways of the world.

I arrived at the government agency in a state of dread. I was expecting a major bureaucratic wrestling match, a battle royale in which a dull, dead-eyed functionary would drag me through acres of forms before sadistically telling me that the dates I wanted were not available. A different date? Oh, you'll have to fill out a new set of forms. Yes, you must start all over. So sorry.

I was expecting to fail. I was anticipating enduring a morning's worth of mental torture. But no, the big man behind the desk was pleasant, helpful, jovial even. And when he sorrowfully informed me that my bag of money was not quite big enough (I'm mathematics impaired and had miscalculated the dollars to shillings conversion), he seemed to suffer a little along with me. Then he carefully directed me to the closest branch of my bank and said we could pick up where we left off when I returned — "No problem." I got to the bank, made the withdrawal — I was then carrying 2 million Uganda shillings in small, unmarked bills (about a thou in U.S. dollars) -- and came back. He was sitting there waiting for me. I plopped down in the chair in front of his desk.

"Are you back?" he said.

"I am," I said.

He checked the date I'd asked for. He smiled. "Excellent, plenty of room!" I think he was as happy as I was. "Who knows, it might be just you two and the guide. That happens sometimes. And them, of course."

"Them" would be the relatives we're going to visit at the end of May. The big, hairy, smelly, quite distant, but nonetheless endearing and charming relatives that live way up in the thickly jungled mountains of Bwindi Impenetrable Forest in southwest Uganda: the mountain gorillas. They are mountain gorillas so there is considerable slippery, slidey, steep, sometimes rainy, hot and buggy hiking involved — it can be as much as eight or nine miles, I've heard. And then, there they are. You spend just an hour with them, and back down the mountain you go. They need their privacy. Plus, they bore easily.

My new best friend did some more checking of this and that on his computer. He asked to see my passport. He carefully filled out the two permits, then he counted the two large stacks of money I had placed in front of him. I was 10 thousand shillings short. I put another 10 thousand shilling note on the desk. He stretched a rubber band around the cash and slipped it into a drawer. He stamped the permits and officiously scribbled something on each one. Then he solemnly handed them to me one at a time.

"The gorillas will be waiting for you," he said. "Don't disappoint them."

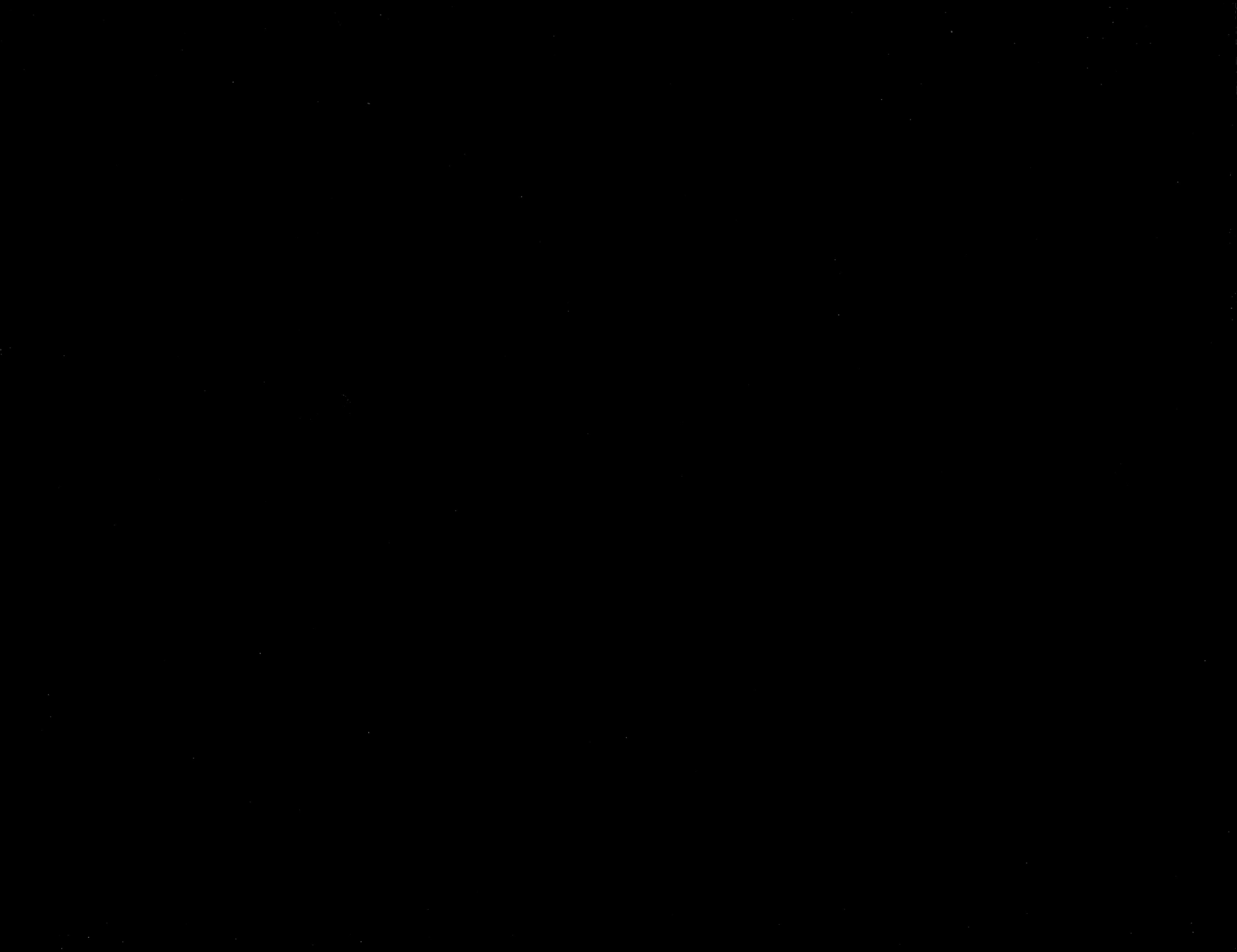

2 FEBRUARY 2010

Chiaroscuro With Your Obundu?

I went to dinner at Enos' home last night. It was the first time I'd been out late in the village. The place was cloaked in deep darkness, but it was a miniature city of lights: Paris, circa Louis XIII. I navigated past fires, through squadrons of fireflies, between green glowing cellphones that seemed to be floating down the pathways on their own, and brushed by shadowy figures carrying high-intensity lavender flashlights that resembled the headlamps of expensive cars. Up in the sky there were half a dozen shooting stars with long yellow trails behind them like the glowing tail feathers of great prehistoric birds.

After work I'm ready for a shower, food, writing, lounging around, reading and not much else. But Enos had come to my office in the morning specifically to ask me to dine with his family. I couldn't refuse. Besides, I like him; he's got a good heart and an easy laugh. We met shortly after I arrived in the village because he operates the carpentry workshop across the road that trains young people, and I needed some shelves made. Lately, I've been helping him write a grant to one of the foreign embassies in Kampala for new tools.

With the dim light I was holding it was hard to see the few steps up to Enos' house, then his wife swung a kerosene lamp out the door and I climbed up to a small room with a low table in the middle. A hanging white sheet cut the room in half. There was a bed behind it. As my eyes adjusted, several posters of the Rwenzori king, the Omusinga, appeared on the opposite wall. Another poster featured portraits of all the Ugandan presidents since the country's 1962 independence.

Biira, Enos' wife, and his sister-in-law, Loyce, took several bowls from a shelf next to the door and placed them on the table — goat meat, pasta, obundu (a sticky, malleable cassava flour dumpling used to sop up the goat broth), and chunks of po-po (papaya). The food was good, but the main attraction was the light, or lack of it.

It was if I'd been invited to spend the evening in an old master painting. Out the open door, a child walked into the blackness carrying a candle, and as she moved across the yard, faces of more children, huddling and staring, emerged from the dark then retreated back into it. Meanwhile, inside where we were sitting it was a three-dimensional Rembrandt. Biira and the baby were in deep shadow on their left, and sprayed with the glow of the kerosene lamp on their right. Enos, his back to them, his dark face to me, was thinly outlined in orange. Loyce, sitting to my right, halfway across the room, appeared to be made of highly polished black marble, her cheeks, nose, chin and forehead glistening with nacreous light.

When it was time to go, Loyce and Enos escorted me all the way back to my house, which is the Ugandan custom: You always walk your guests home. The fires had dimmed by then, the fireflies were still around, but they seemed sluggish, less Tinker Bell-like, and the cellphones had all but disappeared. The only flashlight was mine, which was fading quickly. We spoke hardly at all as we moved through the village. We were spellbound by the beauty of the night, lost in our thoughts, full and weary.

2 FEBRUARY 2010

Speaking in Tongues

Stephen is beating the hell out of Satan. He is whipping him. He is stomping on him. He is shoving the devil out of this world. "Hallelujah!" Stephen says, and the church says, "Amen." A victorious smile illuminates his face. The congregation is with him. He's got Satan on the run.

It's Sunday morning and I've returned to Wakiso for the first time since I left this small town near Kampala in mid-October to move across the country. I go straight from the taxi park to the church. I know Stephen and his family will be there. As I enter, Stephen, without missing a fiery beat, switches from Luganda to English, so I can understand the sermon, and his son Nicholas, also a preacher, steps beside him to translate into Luganda for the rest of the parishioners. They are terrific together, playing off each other, acting out the narrative, Stephen occasionally correcting Nicholas' translation. They're a gifted duo, jamming in the name of the Lord.

For 10 weeks after I arrived in Uganda I lived with Stephen, a Pentecostal minister, his wife, Josephine, two of their sons, the sons' wives and six grandchildren. Stephen and I became good friends. It's an unlikely friendship because we are about as philosophically, spiritually and ideologically different as two people can be. But without ever making a conscious effort to do so, we did not let our diametrically opposite views stop us from talking into the evening by kerosene lamp, strolling through the village, vegetable gardening together, razzing each other about who ate the most, discussing politics or watching the endless, polychrome parade walk past his front porch as the rain and wind blew in from the north.

After church, I walk back to the family home with Nicholas, husband of Grace, and father of Elijah (who's so much bigger than when I last saw him; a little boy now, not a baby). When we arrive, Isaac, Nicholas' brother, and Linda, Isaac's wife, are sitting in the courtyard of the house with their infant daughter. She was born the day after Christmas and she's already rockin' a major crop of hair on her tiny head. Linda nurses her as we stand around, make small talk, take each other in to make up for the time we've been apart. The older kids, shy after three months of not being around me, steal glances, watch from a distance.

Josephine, Stephen and I move inside the house to share a meal of posho (a dumpling-like steamed bread made from maize flour), beans and chapati. Stephen talks about his hopes for the Glorious Grace Church, a "false prophetess" in the area who he says lured away some of his congregation, and his plans to buy a farm.

Being in this home is both foreign and familiar. As Stephen talks, I glance back and forth from his face to Josephine's. She adores him.

And why not? He's funny, charming and, though he's not without an edge, genuinely kind. At one point he says, in reference to her, "We are not two people, we are one person." She laughs and looks down, then nods in agreement, says something indecipherable.

I'm reminded of the many evenings the three of us spent together talking like this, sitting in the darkened living room, gospel radio supplying the soundtrack. They would usually continue to talk long after I'd gone to bed. The prayers from the mosque across the road might go on for an hour or two after that, then, finally, quiet. Until 3 or 4 in the morning. Most nights, that's when I'd hear it: an odd, eerie sound, a sound that I became accustomed to, soothed by over time. At first I'd thought I was dreaming it, but I wasn't. I'd forgotten about it until coming back for this visit.

I usually wake up for an hour or so in the middle of the night, and that has not changed since I've been in Africa. I lie in the dark, use it as a time to meditate on things big and small, happy and sorrowful, mysterious and banal. True to form, my third or fourth night after moving into Stephen and Josephine's I was lying awake, gazing into the blackness. Other than a small dog choir tuning up a few miles away, the night was nearly silent. A hot breeze fluttered the curtains. Then, through the wall came a strange, otherworldly sound, a rhythmic chanting, an incantation being voiced in a dialect I did not recognize. And as I listened more intently, I was sure it was not Luganda. It was definitely not English. It was passionate, pleading, at times fierce and angry, but I couldn't make out a word of it. And then I recalled what Stephen had told me the day I'd arrived, when he was showing me around, explaining the routines. "You may hear me at night," he said. "Sometimes I get up and come into the living room. You might hear me talking to God in a special language."

6 FEBRUARY 2010

The Well-Balanced Life

In some parts of the world – Africa, South America, Asia – people commonly walk around with all sorts of things balanced on their heads. In other parts of the world they don't. Why, I was wondering at 5 in the morning, has that habit evolved in some places, but not in others?

You won't see an elderly, nicely dressed woman walking through Denver with a machete teetering on her noggin. Or an ax. Or a 10-foot-long plank. Or a large plastic basin holding a mountain of flour. Yet dozens of times a day I see women of all ages, and children and men too, walking down the road with most anything you can imagine balanced on their heads. The other day it was a woman with a classic, old black and gold Singer sewing machine. Then there are purses, jackfruit, giant bunches of green plantains, a stack of chapatis, neatly folded linens, shovels, hoes, bundles of firewood, bags of charcoal and, perhaps one of my best sightings, a soldier, obviously on his way home, with his automatic rifle riding atop his felt beret. I'm guessing that's against regulations.

It's an extremely practical technique. If you're a female head balancer, and the majority are, it not only leaves your arms and hands free, it also leaves your back free, and it's a good thing because there's a baby sleeping there much of the day. Some people roll up part of a banana leaf and make a cranium-size loop out of it to facilitate their balancing act. Others do the same with a piece of cloth. Most just put whatever they need to transport up there and there it stays.

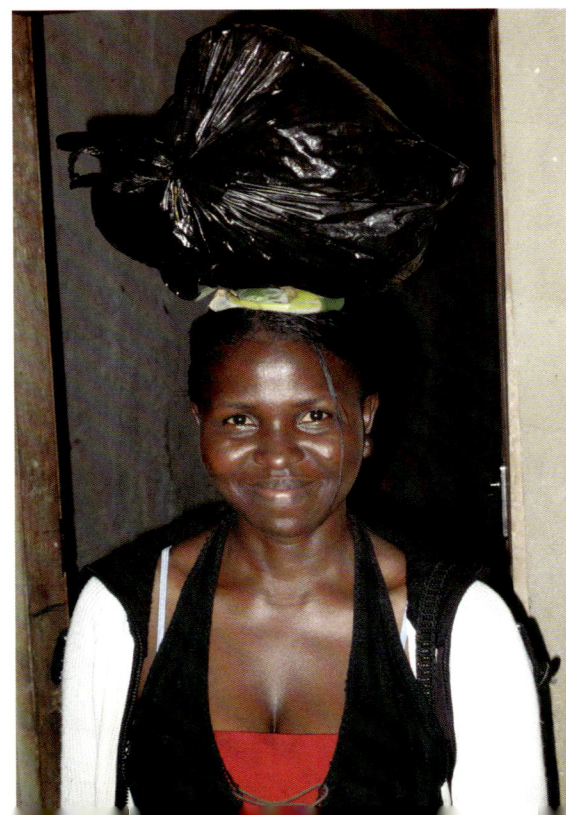

One evening when I was still living near Kampala I was sitting out in the courtyard of the house when Grace, Elijah's mom, got home from work. I could barely see her coming through the shadowy garage, then she appeared in the doorway. On her head was a big plastic bag full of I don't know what. "Duck," I said, pointing to the bag, "or that won't make it through." For some reason, that struck Grace as extravagantly funny. "Go get your camera," she told me. "Make a photo of me!" It reminded me of something my old friend Cese used to say when she'd suddenly find herself experiencing one of life's ordinary but exalted moments, "Quick, take a picture of me. I'm as happy as I'll ever be."

14 FEBRUARY 2010

Invisible Africa

In the spring of 2009, after I learned that I'd be moving to Uganda and started telling friends and family, I'd get one of three responses, or sometimes the whole trinity in quick succession: "Idi Amin," "Ebola," "gorillas." Through no fault of my own, I know a lot of bright, sophisticated, well-read, well-informed people in the U.S., many of whom are media professionals, and yet those three topics were the only ones the vast majority of them associated with this country, and apparently the only things most of them knew about the place. I didn't know much more myself. I'd actually been reading up on Rwanda, as I thought I might be going there, so I'd accidentally acquired what was perhaps marginally more information than the average person has about Rwanda's neighbor nation. But, really, I was largely ignorant about the land that Winston Churchill called the "Pearl of Africa." (It's a phrase invoked ad tedium by every travel brochure, website and blog, where Uganda gets mentioned. Hasn't anyone ever said anything else quotable and positive about this ravishingly beautiful place?)

Idi Amin has been gone from Uganda for more than 30 years. He died in 2003. He came back to life — virtually — in the 2006 film "The Last King of Scotland." The first outbreak of the usually fatal hemorrhagic fever Ebola occurred in 1976 in the Democratic Republic of Congo, then called Zaire. Later, there were outbreaks in Sudan and Cote d'Ivoire. From November 2007 to February 2008 the virus was found in a single district in Uganda, where it infected 149 people, 37 of whom died.

Gorillas, mountain gorillas in the case of Uganda, are large, shaggy, intelligent and altogether charming creatures gifted with deep, dark, poignantly expressive eyes. They're a positive association for any country where they live and Uganda is justly proud of the few hundred who reside here. The fact that there are only about 700 mountain gorillas left on the planet is profoundly sad, but the attention lavished on them in recent years may be the best hope for the species' survival. (The substantial amount of money they pull in for the Uganda Wildlife Authority also bodes well for their continued existence. People, like myself, who shell out the required fee to spend a single hour in the company of mountain gorillas pay at about the same rate they would for a Wall Street lawyer or front seats at a big arena rock concert.)

But none of the above exists in the place I've started to become familiar with since moving here. You won't find gorillas (or lions or giraffes or hippos) or Idi Imin or Ebola in Invisible Africa. Nor will you find draconian, homophobic laws (and pending laws), or genocide or mass rapes or child soldiers or thugs like Lord's Resistance Army leader Joseph Kony and the Janjaweed militia. You will find those things everywhere and repeatedly in the increasingly pervasive media emanating from the developed countries. But Invisible Africa is very rarely seen on CNN, Fox News, BBC, Sky News, in the New York Times, Newsweek, Time, the Economist, Der Spiegel, Le Monde, etc.

Invisible Africa did show up recently, however, in this small mountain village where I'm living. It walked right through the gates of the office compound where I spend most of my days. In fact, it walked through more than 200 times, in the form of coffee farmers, mostly women, who came to attend the annual shareholders meeting of their cooperative and celebrate its 10th anniversary. More of their fellow shareholders, nearly 5,000 of them, couldn't make the get-together, but they come by regularly to do banking at their own savings and loan, make a loan payment, buy shares, pick up new coffee trees at their 100,000 tree nursery, or participate in a workshop on organic farming methods, business planning or how to improve their relationship with their spouse. Their cooperative and its many programs, trainings and workshops is not unique. Similar organizations exist all over Uganda and throughout much of Africa. But CNN, BBC, the New York Times, Newsweek, the Economist and other echo chambers have done an excellent job of keeping such things a secret. Indeed, all manner of good things are going on in Africa, but you're not likely to find out about them in the mainstream media of the first-world countries.

Africa is too rich a resource of tragedy porn, it is too easy for intellectually lazy media makers to typecast it as an ongoing horror movie, a never-ending train wreck, to bother with depicting it as the complex, rich, nuanced place that it is. It has its dark side, to be sure (what place doesn't?), but its societies are gracious, its people kind and funny, sharp and perceptive. It's a land of deep compassion and, given the legacy of a brutal slave trade and colonialism in many of Africa's countries, it is an amazingly buoyant, forgiving, hope-filled place. Every country has its sorrows, every continent is sometimes shadowed by clouds of evil, but it seems that nowhere gets its problems publicized with quite the vigor and enthusiasm that Africa does.

Nor is a Pollyanna-ish, good-news-only approach desirable or useful. A journalist such as Nicholas Kristof, for example, is doing a brilliant, admirable, necessary job of continually calling attention to Africa at its worst. And Richard Dowden certainly doesn't gloss over Africa's shortcomings, yet he also doesn't depict it as having nothing more to offer than shortcomings. Those two -- and there are a handful of others producing good, multi-dimensional work -- understand this place, they get it, they love it, they want the best for it. As for their many colleagues who do not, the greatness of Africa, that is to say most of it and most of what goes on here, is apparently invisible to them, and consequently to the millions of people who rely on them to convey a full, honest depiction of this continent.

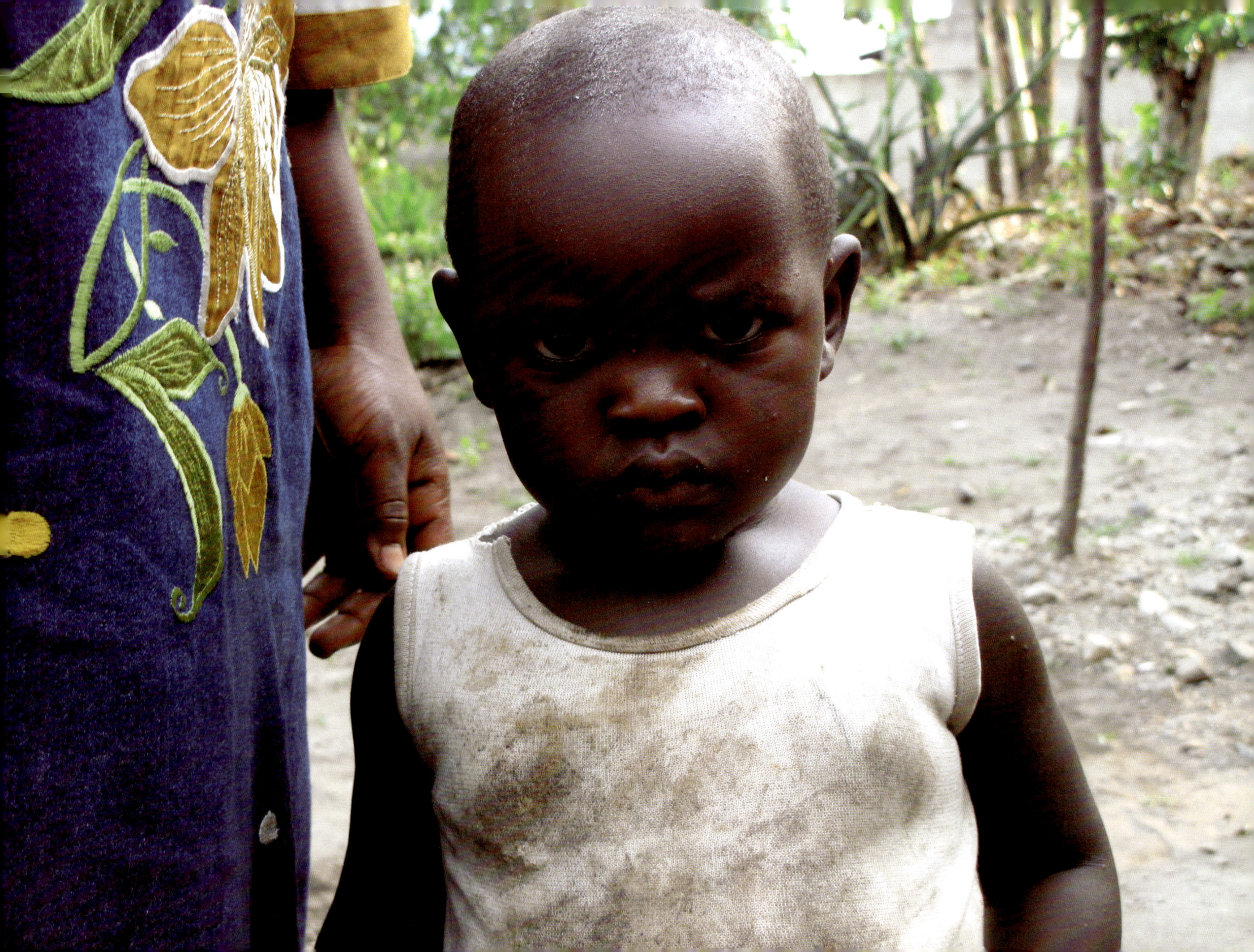

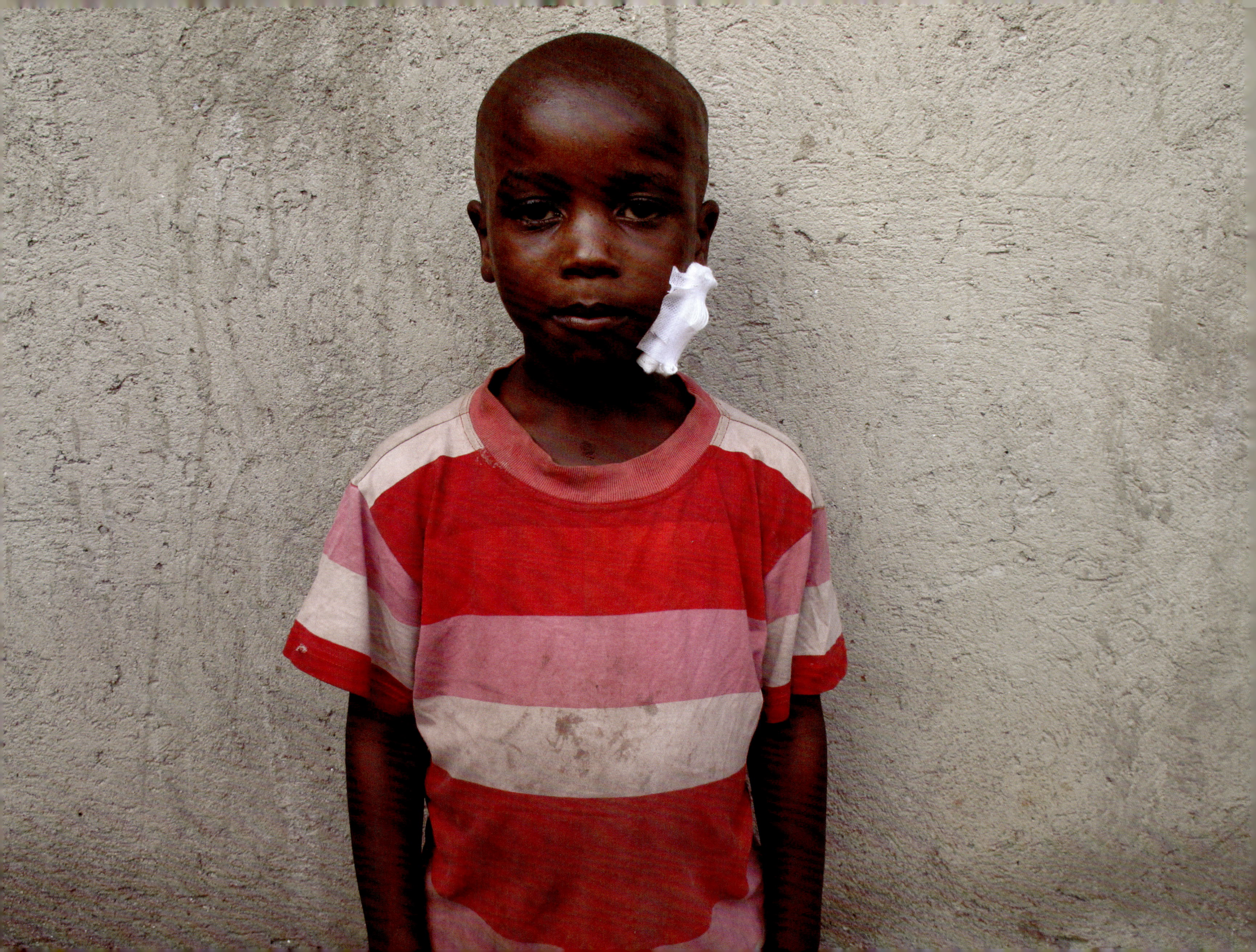

20 FEBRUARY 2010

Riding With Sheena

We're deep into hour five of the seven-hour Kampala-to-Kasese express bus trip, endurance marathon and torture regimen. Express means the bus stops every 15 minutes instead of every 10 minutes. Sometimes it pulls over to pick up or drop off passengers, sometimes it comes to a halt for reasons that shall forever be a mystery. At one stop I look out to see what's being loaded into the luggage compartment. It's a large cow head, horns and all, that was very recently separated from the rest of the cow. Then we're off again.

I'm seated two-thirds of the way back, gazing out into the thick, tangled green of Kibale Forest, a place known for its abundance of chimpanzees and other primates, and approximately a gajillion different species of birds. I'm entertaining myself by keeping a count of the black-and-white colobus monkeys perching in the extremely tall, gangly trees and another of the beehives attached to the trees' trunks and branches. My score so far: eight monkeys, 22 beehives.

The monkeys are easy to spot. They sport a distinctive black-and-white color scheme and a long dramatic tail with a white flare at the end that they like to provocatively hang off the branch they're sitting on. The beehives are a little tougher to ID, but once you train your eye, they are everywhere. They look like big brown bumps. If the bus slows and there's a hive close to the highway, I can see the bees swirling around it, admiring their elevated architectural masterpiece and trying to decide which flame-red flower to buzz over to next. Being a bee in the jungle is all about choice.

I'm hoping to god the driver took his antidepressants this morning because he's driving this mammoth green bus like it's a Lamborghini Miura. He's taking the corners as if he's astride a Vincent Black Shadow. But there's little point in hand-wringing or vocalizing about it because the Afro-pop, hip-hop music videos playing on the TV up front are cranked up to such ear-hemorrhaging volume that — just like in space — you can't hear yourself scream.

Then everything stops and all is silent ...

Suddenly, without reason, without warning, without logic, all of us in the bus are immersed in the chaos of a massive collision. No, no, not that kind of a collision. We haven't hit anything. The driver is piloting this internal combustion leviathan as if there's no tomorrow and it's 30 seconds to midnight, but somehow, in violation of all the laws of physics, he's keeping it on the road and avoiding abrupt contact with other objects, both stationary and mobile. No, what we've suddenly found ourselves immersed in is one of the most exquisite (also embarrassing, absurd, uncomfortable, surreal, awkward) cross-cultural collisions I've been party to since arriving in this glorious land.

The Afro-pop, hip-hop videos have come to a shrieking halt, Radio and Weazel are taking a breather to polish their sunglasses, and in their place, for the entertainment and diversion of the bus's captive audience racing through the rain forest, now comes 1984's stunning cinematic achievement "Sheena," based on the comic "Sheena: Queen of the Jungle." There it is up on the small screen, starring noted thespian, breastian and "Charlie's Angels" alumnus Tanya Roberts. Naturally, the attention of every passenger including me is super-glued to the screen from the film's first frames.

I immediately identify with Sheena for several reasons. 1) We're both in the middle of a rain forest where there's no shortage of chimps and other assorted wild beasts; 2) as the film's prologue tells us, after her parents were killed while on safari, the blond-haired, blue-eyed toddler Sheena was taken in by the kindly Zambuli tribe and mothered by its shaman lady (those of you who know me will immediately recognize the parallels to my own personal history); 3) Sheena is the lone white girl in Zambuli land, while I'm the solitary muzungu on the bus.

As an example of the filmmakers' art, "Sheena" is an endless King Solomon's mine of stereotype, recycled plot and jungle movie cliché. The chimps are cute and funny. Omigawd they are such rascals! What will they do next? The shaman who raises Sheena is noble and wise and, of course, clairvoyant, adept at mind-control techniques and kindly; she only uses her powers for good. Likewise, the lions (who behave like house cats, so devoted are they to Sheena) are also noble and wise. The elephants? Yup, noble and wise. Even the pink flamingos are noble and wise (more about them later).

And Sheena, god bless her, the saucy little Tarzanette, grows up to be a combination of MacGyver and Dr. Dolittle, gifted with a physique that would make her a certain first draft choice for the Swedish Bikini Team (if the qualifications also include nobility and wisdom). She wears almost nothing throughout the entire movie except for those scenes in which she wears nothing. Fortunately, the TV is not where the driver can see it, which is the only reason I'm alive to tell this story. In defense of Sheena's recurring nudity, let me just point out that you have to bathe frequently in crystal clear water to have your hair display the body, luster, bounce and sheen that Sheena's does even under some very trying circumstances, such as being strafed by a helicopter gunship.

Apart from all that, my favorite thing about the film is that Sheena is constantly galloping about on a zebra that is clearly a painted horse, zebras being notoriously cranky and impossible to train because they are embarrassed and bitter about their ridiculous appearance. (Proof that god has a perverse sense of humor and maybe a mean streak.)

Needless to say, there are bad guys, and one very bad gal, also given to minimal clothing, whom Sheena must contend with. I think you know that she gets plenty of help from her animal friends. (She summons them by squeezing the center of her forehead and wincing like she's got a king hell migraine.) Obviously, there is a handsome journalist who falls for her big-time, and his portly cameraman pal who provides many achingly funny moments. For example, a huge lion puts its head through the open window of the Land Rover and licks him. Another time he closes his jacket in the door of the Rover. The laffs never stop. OK, they do once, but only briefly -- when the 8-year-old boy sitting in front of me stands up in the aisle and vomits on my shoes. But that is a brief event and in no time all eyes are back on Sheena and the problems she must overcome — much worse than mere barf — to protect the gentle, freedom-loving Zambuli.

The climax, the only one you actually see on-screen, though there are hints of a hot trip to heaven shared by the Queen of the Jungle and Mr. Loverboy Journalist, is when the enemy gal, a real bitch on wheels if you'll excuse my Zambuli, is trying to push Sheena out of a helicopter over the Raging Certain Death Falls. During that scene you could have heard a pin drop (or an 8-year-old upchuck) in that bus if the sound of the helicopter combined with the falls hadn't been deafening.

Anywho, think about it: You're the director-who-shall-remain-nameless of this turkey and by this time you know you've got a real dawg on your hands, though you are comforted by the fact that you've been able to convince your star to wriggle out of her minuscule leatherette bikini enough times that you're guaranteed sales in a large number of ancillary and foreign markets, not to mention cable and video rental, and don't forget posters. Indeed, a quarter-century after the film's release it will be playing to an SRO audience on a bus rolling across Uganda.

Still, while there on location, you and the scriptwriter, David "I have no shame" Newman, are excavating your rich imaginations for a scene that will really be the capper, absolutely blow audiences out of their seats, so you can wrap this POS and go home to Woodland Hills and buy a new BMW. What do you do? Here are some hints: Tippi Hedren, tweet-tweet, squawk.

Yes, that's it! Newman, you're a genius. Get this: Sheena telepathically emails her pink flamingo BFFs. Their wee bird brains have broadband, so they immediately download the message and wing it over to the falls in a Zambuli second. They surround the helicopter — no, better yet, they fly right inside the helicopter and peck the bejesus out of the pilot and push out the Bitch Goddess who was trying to eject Sheena (whose hands are chained together).

Sheena then manages to get out of the whirlybird somehow. I'm not sure how because at that point the 8-year-old boy stands up in the aisle once more and I get ready for a quick avoidance maneuver in case he's going to do the projectile thing again, but instead he gets distracted by the copter exploding into a ball of fire and going into a death spiral over the falls.

When next we see Sheena, she's had time to blow-dry her hair, even though her hands are still chained together (she's a Houdini li'l vixen) and she is addressing the grateful Zambuli people, mostly young women who like to dance topless around bonfires. Screenwriter Newman really had to go deep for Sheena's lines at this point, but deep he did go, and he brought back treasure: "See! See! Even in chains, we can defeat them! Turn your minds back, oh my people. Remember yourselves, a thousand, a thousand moons ago! Bring your bows! Chief Harumba, attack!"

24 FEBRUARY 2010

Erection

In 1971 John Lennon completed an 18-minute film of a hotel being built in London. He created the film by having a stills photographer lock down a camera pointed at the building site for the entire period of the hotel's construction. Pictures were taken at regular intervals each day. Lennon then assembled the resulting sequential images of the hotel going up and reshot them on motion picture film. He called his movie "Erection."

I recall seeing it, or part of it, one night when Lennon and Yoko Ono, who sang on the film's soundtrack, were guests on "The Dick Cavett Show." I've always found Cavett tedious, but he often had terrific guests. The best combination ever was when he had Salvador Dali and Lillian Gish on in 1970. (Dali walked onstage carrying a live anteater and tossed it in Gish's lap, which neither she nor the anteater appreciated. PETA wasn't around yet and the SPCA was not about to tangle with Dali.) Second best ever: Janis Joplin and Gloria Swanson.

When I heard that the coffee cooperative I work for was going to put up a new building in the banana grove behind my home, I thought of the Lennon film. Now every day after work and every afternoon on Saturdays and Sundays, I go out back and shoot photos of the building's progress. I've only missed a few days. The building is rising with impressive speed, especially considering that no power tools are being used. Even the bricks were made by hand.

The structure will house a hulling machine. Hulling of the coffee beans is currently done by hand, and it is laborious, to put it mildly. The dirty little secret of the coffee business is that coffee beans are not beans, they're the seed of a berry. The seed resembles a bean, I'll grant you that. Anyway, to get at the thing we grind and make coffee out of, the outer flesh, or hull, of the berry must be removed. To do so, the berries are usually dried in the sun and then either the living daylights are beaten out of them with a stick or they are poured through a hand-cranked huller, which strips the hulls from the seeds. Either method is a hell of a lot of work, and explains why so many of the women around here have biceps only slightly smaller than Hulk Hogan's

I savor the afternoon stroll to the building site. As soon as I get home, I duck through the small door in the big metal gates at the back of the compound and walk through the banana grove down the dirt road to the construction area. The late afternoon sun bleaches the steep slopes of the mountains and they look even greener than usual, almost fluorescent. On most days Moses has dropped off a big load of bricks to keep the crew of eight or 10 workers supplied. He also brings gravel and sand.

Building sites are heaven for children and there are usually several scrambling about. No one shoos them or shouts at them. They've got the sense to stay out of the way, so they're allowed to climb and squeal and gallop around as they wish. As I approach, I yell, "Wasi-bere!" The crew shouts a response and one of them invariably adds, "You are welcome." The kids rush toward me to have their photos taken. I comply, show them the results, they laugh and walk away. I shoot a dozen or so pictures from various angles at roughly the same positions around the building.

I'm done in 10 minutes and by then no one is paying any attention to me. One day I explained what I was doing and told them about the movie from which I stole the idea. They nodded politely and went back to laying bricks, pouring cement or climbing, squealing and shouting.

You can watch the entire Lennon film on DV Blog or you can find a two- to three-minute excerpt on YouTube (just search "John Lennon Erection film," unless you're shy about such things). The author of DV Blog describes the film's ending like so: It finishes "with a shot of the completed hotel where all the lights were then turned off, leaving a black screen."

The film I'm imagining never ends.

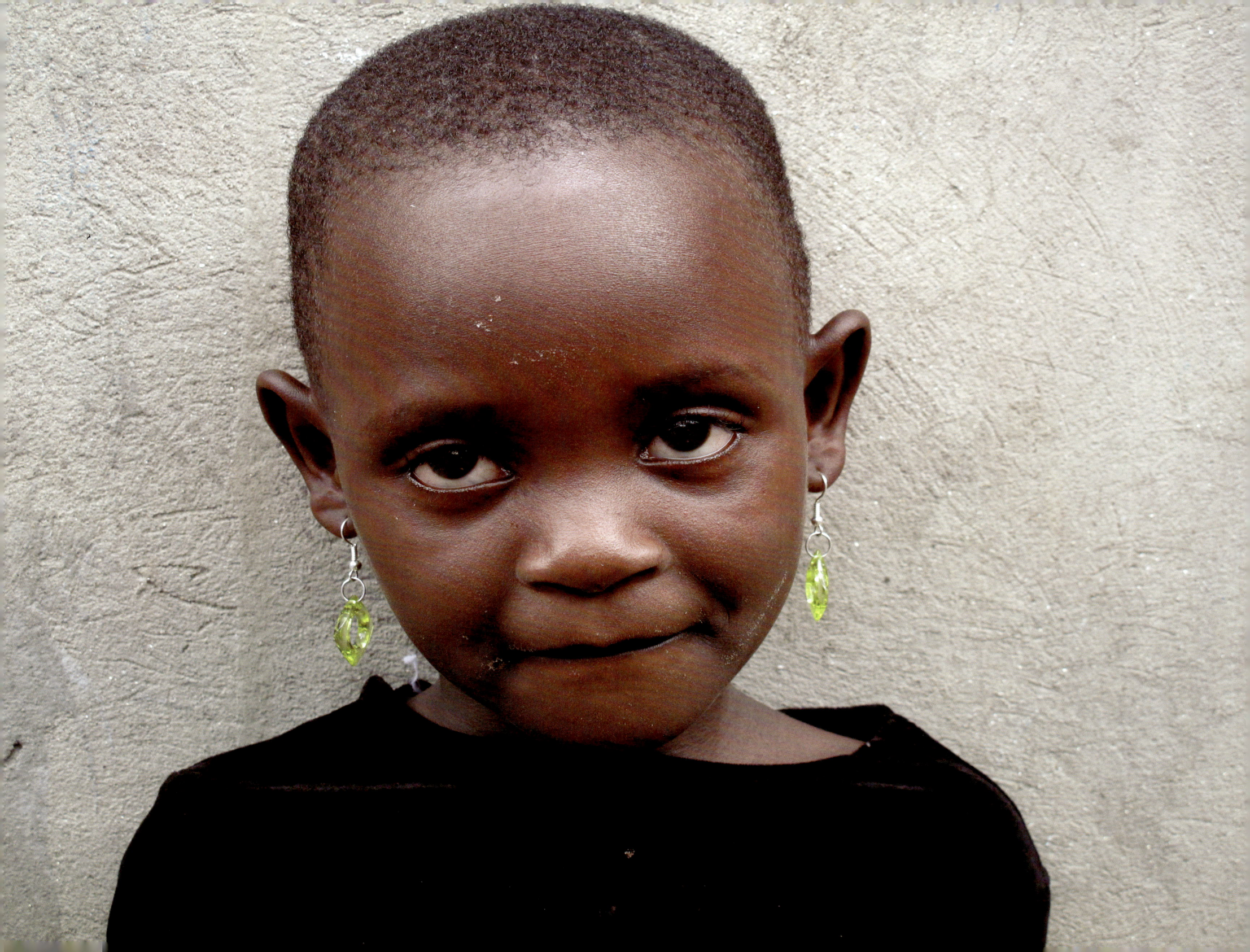

8 MARCH 2010

Madeline Breaks Through

The other day, as I was returning from the shower, I encountered Madeline. She was waddling up and down the courtyard bent in half with part of a gold-color watchband balanced in the center of her small black back. She's 5 or 6 years old and endlessly inventive when it comes to entertaining herself. Later that same day she spent at least three hours exhausting every possibility of what can be done with two metal jar lids. She's not a sunny child. She is shy, observant, pensive and solitary, and seems mildly amused at most everything. I always greet her by name, but she never responds. She watches all that I do with bemused fascination. She is a miniature Mona Lisa with a penchant for arranging and organizing things.

Recently, I noticed a pile of old pill jars, a half-pint waragi bottle, and assorted plastic containers that had been swept into a corner of the courtyard. I thought: Madeline. Twenty minutes later she had them all lined up according to size and height and was deep into an intense pharmacy fantasy, mumbling busily, dispensing a range of invisible potions to a demanding crowd of imaginary customers. "Wabukyrie, Madeline. Yiri wahi?" I said. She glanced at me. She was too busy to talk.

You don't see many toys in rural Uganda, not store-bought toys, anyway. The kids make their own or, like Madeline, simply treat all found objects as recreational opportunities. When I lived near Kampala, I once saw a boy running down the street tugging a long cord. It was tied to a brick that he'd swaddled in a shred of foam, an old piece of mattress. He happily loped up and down the road for an hour or more with that thing whipping and bouncing behind him. Another time, Danny, one of the kids I lived with then, reaped dozens of hours of pleasure from an old broken computer headset. And I regularly come across children with small, elaborate vehicles they've made from bent wire or reeds. The village girls rarely have dolls. By the time they're Madeline's age, most of them have a real baby sister or brother to lug around much of the day. The boys find old motorcycle tires and bicycle rims, or fashion a hoop from a thin branch, then use a stick to chase the wheels through the village, over bridges, up and down trails. Soccer balls, when a real one is not available, which is usually, are made from wadded-up rags wrapped in tape or twine.

Fifteen or so years ago, traveling in Vietnam, I had little kaleidoscopes with me — not the kind with confetti, the ones through which you see multiple images of whatever you point them at. I found the kaleidoscopes at a dime store in Fairfax, Calif. They were a big hit with the rural Vietnamese kids, who I don't believe had seen anything like them, so before I moved to Uganda, I went back to the same store. Still in stock! I bought a dozen or more. I also purchased a bunch of simple wooden tops. On a recent evening I brought out one of the tops and showed Madeline how to spin it. She was entranced. She picked up the technique right away. She was also timid when I told her she could keep it, but I finally coaxed her into taking it from me. Her aunt, Roselin, whom I work with, whose singing I've written about in the past, and who's taking care of Madeline these days, told me her niece played with the toy late into the evening. An excellent ROI.

Early last night, I came out into the courtyard and Madeline was sitting on a stool in front of Roselin wearing a skullcap of soap. "Madeline," I said, "you look like a very old lady with gray hair." She stared at me, silent. Roselin laughed and started shaving Madeline's head with a double-edge razor blade. Many children and grown-ups here wear their hair shaved right to the scalp. It's an ideal style for this weather and it's easy to wash and dry. The razor blade made me nervous, but Roselin wielded it expertly and Madeline sat rock-still, which could not have been easy for her because she's otherwise in constant motion and, like her aunt, singing all the time. When Roselin finished, not one nick.

"Well done," I told Madeline when she was allowed to get up. "I have a reward for you." I went inside my room and got one of the kaleidoscopes. I handed it to her and showed her how to look through it, turning it to rotate the multiple images. She peered through the device for a long time, silently, then looked directly at me and smiled a major, full-power smile.

This morning, once again making the short hike back to my rooms from the shower, there was Madeline, pharmacy freshly stocked with various containers she'd scavenged. To the side, next to a bowl of rice and beans she was having for breakfast, was a platter-size taro leaf with a single, neatly arranged serving: one top, one kaleidoscope. But Madeline was too busy to talk.

14 MARCH 2010

Archeology of a Sunlit Morning

I woke up humming. I was humming in my sleep and continued to hum as I entered consciousness, and as I walked to the latrine, and as I came back to my rooms, and as I went out to the spigot in the courtyard for coffee water, and as I made the coffee. At some point I switched to whistling, my preferred medium. It was a medley, the kind you'd hear on an insipid TV variety show in 1974 with dancers emerging from behind giant, sherbet-colored daisies. It was all sun songs, pretty good songs, though. It probably had to do with yesterday's walk home from work. About 4:30 p.m., following a half-dozen teeth-shaking thunder cracks, the sky stopped sulking and started crying like crazy for an hour or so. The short trek to my rooms was more skating than walking. I stayed on my feet, but just barely. Holiday on mud.

The next morning, sun out, I whistled the Beatles' "Here Comes the Sun" and "Sun King" from the "Abbey Road" album; Bobby Hebb's 1966 R&B hit, "Sunny"; and Shawn Colvin's enigmatic "Sunny Came Home." Over and over. I couldn't stop. It was annoying even to me. Then came a strange craving to hear a song that is not vaguely related to the others, Merle Haggard's howling incantation to the endless highway, "White Line Fever." Where the hellhound did that come from? I couldn't whistle it very well, but I would have liked to hear it just then. Walking to work, I occupied myself with an archaeological excavation of what little remains of my memory. I dug up what I recalled of how those songs entered my life. At first, Haggard's was a mystery. Later the connection became clear.

October 1969. While walking up Telegraph Avenue in Berkeley, stoned out of my 16-year-old gourd, an odd, gurgling riff rumbles out of a record store, followed by the familiar voice of John Lennon shouting unfamiliar, nonsensical lyrics, "Here come old flattop he come grooving up slowly/ He got joo-joo eyeball he one holy roller ..." Before the song ended, I owned "Abbey Road." An hour later, I owned two tabs of Orange Sunshine. A new Beatles album required high-octane accompaniment. A friend and I dropped the Sunshine, took the record back to his place and listened to it all night long.

As we listened and hallucinated, we pored over a book I'd recently been given: the big Salvador Dali coffee table volume with the embossed gold cover, a 10-pound candy box of surrealism filled with the high-calorie works of the master of attention-getting. The Beatles' "Sun King," I decided upon first hearing it, was obviously about Versailles and its creator (that the song's lyrics featured a passage of Portuguese/Italian/Spanish gibberish, not French, slipped past me). Not much of a leap, I suppose: Louis XIV was the Sun King. It was meant literally: He was the source of all that was beneficial, all wealth, all favor, all light and heat. He was the life force of the country, not to mention that he effectively owned all of France and everyone in it.

Louis in his time, like the Beatles in theirs, was, by most accounts, an entity of shimmering brilliance, preternaturally charismatic and appealing. While he ruled, life was good, it was great, it was marvelous, darling — unless you were a peasant; for peasants it was about the same as things always are for peasants. At Versailles, it was chorus after chorus, 24-7, of "Here comes the Sun King/ Everybody's happy/ Everybody's laughing." Yet he was far more than cash and flash. Lord Acton called Louis "the most able man ever born on the steps of a throne."

Looking down from the considerable height of my altered consciousness that long ago teenage evening, the Beatles seemed a glorious multiheaded hybrid, Salvador Dali blended with the Sun King, four monarchs living in a Versailles of the mind, surrounded by surreal auditory paintings of their own invention, lyrically governing their vast kingdom, comprising the vision-hungry, the hedonistic, the hormone-fueled. My lysergic thoughts conflated it all. I vividly pictured an ermine-draped Louis floating through the Hall of Mirrors, looking like a young Dali, a parade of fantastically clothed courtiers and ladies-in-waiting trailing behind him, flirting and stealing glances at their dazzling reflections as they strolled, a sexually charged, hallucinatory procession. Then it was a movie projected in the air before me, a 15th century French Bollywood production choreographed by Busby Berkeley: Louis stops, he turns. All stop with him. They turn, first to the left, then to the right. They spin. They twirl. They freeze. They throw their heads back. They kick one leg out. Louis hotly raps the parquet floor with his ivory inlaid staff. He taps it once. He knocks it twice. He cracks it thrice, he shakes his lush black mane, stamps his red velvet slipper and loudly decrees, "Come together. Right now. Over me."

It's no mystery that Bobby Hebb's "Sunny" was another of the songs sloshing around in my drowsy morning head — if ever there was an antidote to a thunderstorm. Before I ever heard it on the radio I heard "Sunny" sung live by a phenomenally brave Louise Orland — Louise Boredom we called her — at the junior high school talent show. I recall several abysmal versions of "Satisfaction" at that show, but Louise's performance was the mind-blower. Louise, it turned out, was a shape changer. I was 12 at the time and didn't have a clue what that might mean, but something inside remembered and years later, purely by accident, it was confirmed. Louise had that certain something that can't be found in books. The nasty irony is that books were her only friends at the time.

We were all cruel to Louise, mean in the ways that kids can be; merciless. Her nickname was one of the nicer things we did for her. She was not blessed with what we considered acceptable looks or hair or clothes or knowledge of TV shows or speech patterns. She was not interested in the dimwitted topics we were interested in. She was slightly overweight, came from a poor family, wore Buddy Holly glasses, had acne and was intensely cerebral. That she had a deep, dusky, gorgeous soul (and plenty of it) escaped us all. Her dry wit was way over our heads. We should have been ashamed, but of course we were not. We found ourselves to be brilliantly funny and clever. Me and my guy friends, teetering at the threshold of puberty, were ill-equipped to comprehend the authentic sex appeal standing right in front of us. We knew there was something about Louise. But we didn't know what it was. So we made fun of her.

There was a cacophony of catcalls, farting sounds, burps, hoots and shrill whistles when she glided out on that junior high school stage wearing a formal that she'd borrowed. She acknowledged none of it. She was already on Planet Louise. Mr. Weig, the bow tie-wearing, bullhorn-wielding vice principal, finally managed to get us to shut up. A yellow spot lit Louise and her incredible voice illuminated those opening lines:

> *Sunny, yesterday my life was filled with rain.*
> *You smiled at me and really eased the pain.*
> *The dark days are gone, and the bright days are here,*
> *My Sunny one shines so sincere.*
> *Sunny one so true, I love you.*

She owned it and she owned us. She sang that song up one side and down the other. Bobby Hebb would have been in tears if he'd been there. She cast a spell. We were stunned, transported. We knew we were listening to something real, coming from somewhere we'd never been (and many of us would never get to); beyond that we were mired in our usual pre-adolescent cluelessness. Afterward, we weren't all of a sudden nicer to Louise. If anything, we were increasingly wary. She was clearly miles ahead of the rest of us. She was hip while we were still trying to figure out what it meant and how you got it. We didn't know what to do with her.

Like a predictable movie plot, years later I ran into her at a party in L.A. I was working in films and the gathering was at a crew member's house in Laurel Canyon. We were celebrating the last day of shooting some movie or TV show. As you have guessed by now, Louise had changed. She was statuesque, very stylish, very attractive in an understated, upscale bohemian sort of way. I had no idea who she was when we started talking, but her speaking voice was strangely familiar. We got around to discussing where we'd grown up and then figured out we'd both gone to the same junior high school and then, "No! You're Louise Orland? Oh. My. God."

She was extremely kind, claimed that what little she recalled of me was all good. I apologized several times over on behalf of the entire seventh grade's assholishness and raved about her rendition of "Sunny." She said she just barely remembered it. At that point her husband — a George Clooney type, but more handsome than the actor — walked over and joined us, and we recounted the whole weird story for him.

I asked the obligatory question before I departed: "So, what are you doing now?"

"I'm a psychiatrist," Louise said.

"Still sing?"

"Only when driving."

Twenty-odd years after that a friend phoned me and asked me to go to a concert. Who's Shawn Colvin? The name was familiar but I couldn't place her. She did that song "Sunny Came Home." OK, I think I know that one. Want to go or not? It's getting late. I want to ask someone else if you're not interested. She's a folk singer? Right, go or no? Yes, I'll go, sure. You have to drive. OK.

I wasn't expecting much, frankly, but I'd had many good evenings of live music in the old, renovated movie theater where the concert was taking place and I was prepared to have an adult beverage or two and enjoy whatever transpired. Colvin walked onstage to far too much adulation, whistling, applause. She looked out at the audience, smiled and said, "Oh, stop it." She had me at "it." The audience went silent, she sat on a stool and strummed the opening chords of what they all wanted to hear. She sang,

> *Sunny came home to her favorite room*
> *Sunny sat down in the kitchen*
> *She opened a book and a box of tools*
> *Sunny came home with a mission*

I was surprised how much I liked her, surprised at how well-crafted her songs were, at what a solid, authentic musician she was. I was seduced by her sweet-tempered toughness, intrigued by the odd curves her lyrics took, the radical juxtapositions she made when she sang other people's compositions. Her choices were eclectic, at least. And always right. I sat in that theater transfixed, appreciating the concert much more than I'd expected to. We moved up to the balcony for a while, then came back down to the edge of the stage to listen and watch from 8 feet away as Colvin did her final two songs.

The penultimate was one I'd all but forgotten, a hit long, long ago for the much maligned Donovan, he of "Sunshine Superman" (hey, I forgot to whistle that one), "Mellow Yellow" and "Wear Your Love Like Heaven." In his day he was all dreamy, diaphanous, overly sweet; Dylan was dark, trenchant, sharp-tongued. The two were compared at the time of their initial stardom and Donovan suffered. But Colvin redeemed him that night. She gave us an exquisite rendering of his youthful, lovely "Catch the Wind," written when we were all so childlike. The song ends, "For standin' in your heart/ Is where I want to be, and I long to be/ Ah, but I may as well, try and catch the wind."

Luckily I hadn't had more to drink -- it was tough getting to the bar — because I would have drowned out Colvin's next song with my blubbering. Instead, I merely got a little glassy-eyed and stared up at her the way all of us 12-year-old boys should have been staring up at Louise Orland at the junior high talent show if we'd had what my mom called "the brains that god gave a goose."

In fact, I probably couldn't have drowned out Colvin, because moments after she let the word "wind" breeze through the theater until it blew away, she lit into a hard, rough strumming and began a rising, drawn-out howl that slowly, mournfully shaped into "Whiiiiiite Liiiiiiine Feeeeverr …"

What a beautiful shock it was. From Donovan to Merle Haggard. From the ethereal adolescent romanticism of "Catch the Wind" to the hard, haunting ballad of the road, loneliness, growing old, never stopping, always moving. What deep, intelligent imagination it took for Colvin to pair those two. And what a good night it was, so good the whole thing hid out in my subconscious and, years later, followed me all the way to Africa, where it rose one morning with the sun.

26 MARCH 2010

Running Into an Old Friend

In its glory years of 1959-1960 I was a member of the Hayward Public Library Bug Club. I've always had an affinity for insects. The wonderful woman who ran the Bug Club was Gladys Conklin, the children's librarian. She also wrote children's books — about bugs. One of them, "I Like Bugs," was dedicated to me and a friend: "the 6-year-olds in the Bug Club." Many years later Mrs. Conklin, which is what I always called her, got Alzheimer's disease. One day the garden gate was accidentally left open and Mrs. Conklin wandered out. She was never seen again.

She would be happy, I think, to know that I am in Africa, which has plenty of bugs. Some are very strange looking and some are very large, others are exquisitely beautiful and some look good to eat. I've dined on the grasshoppers here. When I lived near Kampala, I had a conversation with Grace, mother of Elijah, about eating insects. It went like this:

Me: I ate some grasshoppers today.

Grace: And ...

Me: Pretty good, tasted like almonds.

Grace: I've never had almonds.

Me: They taste like grasshoppers.

Grace: I want to eat a scorpion. They look so good.

Me: But they're poisonous.

Grace: You take off the poison part.

Me: I knew that.

Then there are the bugs that don't get eaten. They get taken for a ride. Walking home today, I came across two schoolgirls going down the road. As I passed them, I saw that one of the girls had a big grasshopper sitting on top of her head. "Can I take a picture of you and your pet," I asked. "Her?" she said, pointing up to the grasshopper. "Sure, I forgot she was up there." I took the shot, showed it to the girls, riotous laughter ensued. I think I heard a tiny snicker come from the grasshopper. Perhaps her name was Mrs. Conklin.

5 APRIL 2010

Driving a Soft Bargain

"The Scot never took with you," my father was fond of telling me. He was right. I'm of Scottish descent but I'm not thrifty, I'm not a bargainer, I don't care about saving money. I understand the logic of it; it's just not a form of logic I've ever embraced. I don't go wantonly throwing money around — especially these days — but it doesn't matter to me what I pay for something I want. And in my current circumstances bargaining, though everyone insists I must, is something I can bring myself to do only when the price being asked is so utterly beyond reason that I am compelled to challenge it or lose what little self-respect I still possess. Also, by not bargaining I save a hell of a lot of time. And time, as Boy George so eloquently put it lo those many years ago, "makes lovers feel like they've got something real."

One of the holy tenets contained in the casual advice and official indoctrinations you receive when moving to Africa is that you have to bargain in the marketplace. You must do so with street vendors, with touts, shopkeepers and transport purveyors. Whatever it is they're asking for, make them take less. Because, if you don't, it could reflect on you very poorly, word will get out and you, and every visitor who follows you, will be endlessly taken advantage of, overcharged and cheated in perpetuity. What's more, international relations for the balance of the 21st century will suffer irreparable damage.

Really? What if I don't care? What if I don't want to?

And I never do. So I initiated my own foreign aid program shortly after arriving here. It's an on-the-ground, one-on-one, direct assistance, no-waiting, immediate delivery plan that goes like this: Whether it's a bunch of bananas, a chicken or a pair of flip-flops, I pay the asking price, which is often astonishingly cheap, sometimes fantastically inflated, but much of the time perfectly reasonable. Innovative? To be sure. A sweeping disservice to fellow First Worlders? Perhaps. Revolutionary? Ya think?

Sometimes I even throw in a bonus. (Tipping is usually not done here.) On Saturday I was picked up by a taxi driver named Saturday. "It's my birthday today," he said. "I have a birthday once a week." He was charm incarnate with the accent of a BBC announcer, and a careful driver to boot. "You sound like a BBC announcer," I told him. "I wish I was one," he said. When he dropped me off, I asked him to return two-and-a-half hours later and pick me up. He was punctual to the minute. He got a 50 percent windfall.

Bargaining has been one of the inviolable laws of travel and residence by foreigners in third-world countries ever since I can remember and no doubt long before that. For some reason it is considered terribly important for those of us who are exorbitantly flush compared to most of our fellow humans on this rotating vale of tears to journey to the poverty-stricken corners of the world and see how little money we can give its people. For some, it's sport. But, like bullfighting, I'm not certain all the participants enjoy it equally. Some have more at stake than others.

People don't travel to the Champs d'Elysee or Rodeo Drive or the Ginza or Saville Row and browbeat shopkeepers in an effort to reduce their income (which is likely exorbitant). Why do it in Lima or Kampala or Hanoi, or the multitude of tiny electricity-free, mud hut villages where billions of people are attempting to scratch out a living? Aren't those the places where we should be spending as much money as possible instead of as little as we can?

8 APRIL 2010
Crossing Kampala

There is depraved irony in the fact that one of the main boulevards running through Kampala's tony Nakasero neighborhood, home to numerous foreign embassies, foreign aid agencies and the Uganda headquarters of many foreign corporations, is Lumumba Avenue. Hopefully the ghost of Patrice Lumumba has a bent sense of humor. How could you survive as the ghost of Patrice Lumumba if you did not? (Lumumba, the Republic of Congo's first democratically elected prime minister after the nation freed itself from Belgium's long and brutal dominance, was in office mere weeks before there was a coup. Not long after that he was murdered -- with the likely complicity of foreign governments, namely Belgium and the United States.)

Irony and international skulduggery notwithstanding, Lumumba Avenue was where I was picked up by Steven. "Call me Steven Taxi," he instructed as I typed his name and number into my cellphone. "That way whenever you need a taxi you'll think of me." Most of Kampala's cabbies are ace raconteurs and at least as gifted at conversation and banter as London cabbies, and the Ugandans' stories tend to have greater range.

We didn't have far to drive, but it was rush hour and Kampala traffic was more insane and sluggish than usual if such a thing is even possible (in our 20-minute crossing of the city we saw two motorcycle accidents and a half-dozen near misses). Steven filled the time by talking and I filled the time by making notes and taking pictures. "Yes," Steven continued, "you and I must work together. If you need a taxi, you call me. I will come get you anywhere in the city, no charge, and take you wherever you have to go at a very fair price, very fair."

"Can't beat that," I said. "I've got your number." And I held the phone up so he could see his number was entered under Steven Taxi.

"Where are you from?" he asked.

"USA. California."

"Did you vote for Obama?"

"I did."

"Was it a miracle he got elected?"

"Yeah, it was," I said. "I didn't believe it even in the weeks leading up to the election when the polls had him way out in front. I assumed something would happen."

"An October surprise," Steven said.

"Where did you learn that term?" I asked.

"I lived in the U.S. for seven years."

"Really, where?"

"New York. I used to read a lot. That's what I did for fun, the only fun thing."

I asked him what he'd liked best and least about the U.S. Before he answered, he told me he'd worked in a gun factory, a factory that made police pistols. He worked on the loading dock, loading trucks all night long. He made very good money, he said, and was able to send a lot of it home to his wife and four kids, and when he returned to Uganda he bought two taxis and two houses. "All I did was work and eat and sleep. No drinking, no nightclubs, no women, nothing. Seven years."

"You've got a lot of discipline."

"But there was a sad part," he said.

"What was that?"

"I was gone too long. My wife kept asking me to come back, but I wanted to make more money. I didn't even come back to visit. So she

was unfaithful and now we are no longer together. You see, I was illegal. I had a three-month visa, but I stayed, so I couldn't leave if I wanted to get back in."

"I'm sorry about your wife," I said.

"I understand it from her side," he said. "But the kids are mad at her. I tell them no, they must love her because she is their mother, and she took care of them when I was gone. It's OK. 'If it's OK,' they tell me, 'why don't you get back together?' It could happen, but I don't think so."

"You have the kids?"

"Yes, I have all four: two boys, two girls, oldest is 17. I am a good father to them."

"So," I said, "thing you liked least about the U.S., then thing you liked best?"

Steven thought for a long moment until he was distracted by the first of the two motorcycle accidents. No injury to the driver, but the bike had to be carried off the field of battle. Once we'd adequately discussed the calamity, Steven returned to my question.

"I guess the thing I liked least was the African-Americans," he said.

"Suvamo?" I said, using the Lhukonzo word for "repeat that," which I immediately realized meant nothing to Steven because he's a Luganda speaker. "What did you say?"

"The African-Americans, they were terrible to us. When we walked home, they would throw things from the roof. And once they came to our apartment and pulled a gun and said, 'Give me your money.' I did not like them at all. They would say, 'Go back where you came from. You come here and take our jobs.'"

"What parts of New York did you live in?"

"Brooklyn, Bronx, Queens. In Brooklyn people were nicer."

"How'd the white people treat you?"

"They were nicer than the African-Americans, except I found a church I wanted to go to, a house of God. It was all whites and me. They made it very hard on me."

"How so?"

"I thought I should just be able to walk in and sit down and worship."

"Yeah, I think that's the way it's supposed to be with churches."

"They said if I wanted to join I'd have to complete a lot of requirements, a very high number of requirements, many requirements, lots of them ..."

"Got it," I said.

"I'd have to fill out many papers and ..."

"They were going to make it so much trouble to join that you wouldn't want to."

"Right."

"So the blacks weren't very nice, the whites weren't either. The U.S. is a big country. Everyone isn't like that. I'm sorry you weren't treated well. People have been very good to me in Uganda."

"Ugandans love muzungus!" Steven said. "When you come here, we treat you very well. We are happy to see you."

"I know. Everyone has been great. I have no complaints."

"What complaints?"

"No, I said I have no complaints. I like it here."

"Oh, I thought you said you had complaints."

There was a long pause as the conversation recovered from that minor spinout and Steven eased the taxi around the nose of a stalled truck that was almost completely blocking the road, and about which four men were in deep discussion, though a solution for its removal didn't seem to be imminent.

"The U.S. was OK," Steven said. "I brought home a lot of money."

"And you lost your wife."

"Yes, that was the sad thing," he said. "Seven years is a long time."

"But it is so expensive to live in New York. How did you manage to bring back money, or to have any left over to send home?"

"It's expensive for you, but when we live there it is not expensive. We had nine of us in a one-bedroom apartment. We ate Chinese food every night. I could get a big container of fried rice for $2. That was what I had for dinner every night. And I never went out. I worked, came home, ate, went to bed."

"Do you think you'll ever go back, just for a visit?"

"No," Steven Taxi said. "I think I'm comfortable here."

"And what was the best thing about the U.S., the thing you liked the most?" I asked.

"The freedom," Steven said, "the freedom ... and 'Wrestlemania.'"

24 JUNE 2010

Somehow

There are more than 50 languages spoken in Uganda, but English is the country's official one. However, over the years, Ugandans have made an English that is largely their own, and in doing so have imbued it with poetry and considerable charm, a trait they possess in abundance.

To do something methodically, cautiously, is to do it "slowly by slowly."

"How's there?" is an inquiry as to the general state of things in the place you just came from.

"How's here?" asks about the situation in the place you are standing.

To want something right away is to want it now now. You wish to leave immediately? Let's go now now. It is one of the perfect constructions in Ugandlish. Can there be any doubt what it means? No no.

Now now also describes the prevailing mind-set here. Everything is now now. If I tell someone, "Yes, I'd like to come visit your farm sometime," they reply, "OK, let's go." There is no later. The present is where we are. It's what is, the only thing that is. The past is gone. The future may arrive any minute (or never), but it's not here now now.

Speaking of time, if you want to know how things have been going for someone in the recent past, she will likely respond, "Somehow."

It's hard to imagine a more accurate answer than that.

26 JUNE 2010

Fraternizing With the Charismatic Mega Fauna

In that day's most moving moment, Regina, one of the porters, turned to me, pointed way down the hill at two furry black blobs in the chartreuse brush at the bottom of the steep tea field, and said, "You will be the last to reach them, so you should be the first to see them." She was correct on both counts. The young, athletic members of our group were well ahead of us, but they had not yet spotted the mountain gorillas. For a few moments, it was just me and Regina and a couple of magnificent great apes with the lush tapestry wall of Bwindi Impenetrable Forest as backdrop.

Once down among them, we saw more, a dozen. Another six could be heard in the nearby woods. We were very impressed with them. They were very interested in eating leaves. On a couple of occasions one of the adult females came within a meter of where we were standing; close enough that I could briefly look into her dark amber eyes. She looked back at me, gazed intently, blinked and moved on. At one point, the massive silverback, the alpha male, let out a low, ominous gargling sound. "We should back up a little," one of the guides said.

"He thinks we're too close." And our entire group stepped back promptly, like a well-rehearsed dance routine.

The babies were clownish. One kept climbing up a sapling too thin to hold its weight. When it got two-thirds of the way up, the young tree would bend over and dump the little ape on the ground. He'd climb it again. It would drop him again. And so on.

The silverback seemed to crave solitude; he'd eat for a while then lean back and stare dreamily up at the sky in a slightly stoned reverie.

Their human-like qualities are too often commented on. What's truer is their remarkable otherness: so close, yet so far. That, after all, is what makes being near them so bittersweet. We are drawn to them, but we can never really intersect. We can see them but we can't reach them. They are there and we are here. The genetic chasm is unleapable. Besides, as handsome, dignified and thrilling to behold as they are, their main interest is eating leaves.

5 JULY 2010

Blues Dog Bites

One of the extraordinary qualities I've found in the people here — and I suspect it's common elsewhere in Africa as well — is the unique ability to laugh at that which most of us would consider profound tragedy. It's a gift, an amazingly inventive coping mechanism that enables one to withstand huge personal damage or witness horror, then to repair oneself, to move on, largely restored, and to live. It is a means of partitioning sorrow.

The American hipster-humorist Lord Buckley, who died in 1960, saw it in African-Americans and described it this way: "They got themselves a zig-zag way of talking that eventually became their intimate social language. It has a fantastic sense of renewal … Many, many times they had to laugh at a number of things that weren't funny, and as a consequence they wound up with very, very deep sparkling humorous wells of beauty." Buckley called it a "great power — a power that said, everything is understandable."

And if not understandable, perhaps transformable — into something manageable. One aspect of humor, after all, is to take the bite out of pain and misfortune, to remove the sting from heartbreak and calamity.

It is a talent that was brought by Africans to America, brought by the many who willingly and unwillingly immigrated. It was given melody and lyric, chanted and wailed, howled and hooted and hollered, and turned into one of the most expressive, powerful art forms: blues music, a strangely beautiful genre, lusty and loving, hurtful and healing; a never-ending, self-perpetuating collection of incantations that manage to feel good and bad simultaneously. And through its singular nature, the blues — both listening to it and playing it — has helped many a man and woman make it through many a dark night. It is the greatest of medicines.

Not long ago, I was talking to a 40-something Ugandan woman who was sitting one table away from me at a hotel restaurant. She mentioned her daughter. "How old is she?" I asked. "She's gone," she said, and let out a truly lighthearted, joyful giggle. "She died twenty years ago when she was 5, of pneumonia." Her laugh was so out of sync with what she'd said that it really threw me for a moment. I wondered if I'd heard right. "She was very funny," the woman continued. She looked out the window for a moment, melancholy. "Sometimes she liked to pretend she was a dog and bite me, not to hurt, just play biting. She was so funny when she did that. If I was feeling down, it would cheer me right up. I'd laugh so hard." And the thought of it, the recollection of her little girl, two decades gone, pretending to be a dog, transformed her, renewed her. She laughed. And I did too.

12 JULY 2010

Peaking

Saturday morning in the Rwenzori Range, near Congo. Clouds wrap the peaks that emerge from a collar of thick forest. Where the lush trees were long ago cleared, there are grassy fields and crops — cassava, potatoes, groundnuts, matooke, coffee. And the four of us. We are walking single file on a narrow trail. We are on one mountainside, the children are on another. There is a deep valley between us. They watch silently as we walk.

Then comes one of those moments; just a few eternal minutes — a peak experience, literally and figuratively — that will stay as long as memory. Maybe longer.

They yell. We see them. They wave. We wave. They applaud, hands held over their heads. We do the same. We pause, watch them a while longer, wave goodbye, and start to make our way down the mountain.

Then we hear it: They are singing to us, their eight or so child voices swimming through the high African air. And they keep singing as we descend to the valley, the sweet fade of a cappella following us, following us, following us, following us, following us.

23 JULY 2010

It's Only Rock in Road, but I Like It

They're widening a road in the village. I walk over it a couple times a day. I look up one way and down the other to check the progress. Men and women using hoes and shovels are doing the work almost entirely by hand. They've removed some big rocks by digging around them then breaking them up. But they may have met their match with the bruiser they unearthed yesterday. It looks like a bloody meteor crashed to earth. By late this afternoon as I walk home, the monster seems to have grown. The more they dig, the bigger it gets. I'm thinking it could be a giant cork, and when they finally pull it out, the earth will deflate and collapse inward. Just this once, I hope I'm wrong.

30 JULY 2010

Heroic Toy Manufacturers of Uganda

The kids here make most of their own toys. They're extremely good at it. Madeline, one of the little girls who lives in the same compound I do, has made several dolls from small, flat sticks; she draws the faces on them and fashions clothing from rags that she wraps and ties with elaborate sashes torn from scraps of batengi, the gorgeous printed cloth that is everywhere here. Her dolls apparently need a lot of sleep as she is constantly tucking them into their small beds — boxes she's found — in one corner of the courtyard. She then busies herself with a pharmacy assembled from old jars and bottles scavenged here and there. Most of her remedies call for vigorous mixing and shaking of various mysterious compounds. Many get tested on the dolls, which perhaps explains their need for prolonged bed rest.

A couple of weeks ago, during a hike in the Rwenzoris, I came across a boy making bicycles — out of wood. He'd skillfully carve and chisel the entire vehicle. He was just finishing the handlebars for one as I walked up. I watched as he worked, then he demonstrated the bike for me, coasting down a small hill and triumphantly raising his arms over his head when he got to the bottom.

As I was leaving, he asked where I was from. "USA," I said.

"Obama, the hero!" he exclaimed, pointing to his bike. "That's its name!"

2 AUGUST 2010

Stoptime: The Tyranny of Photography

I'm constantly being photographed by people without cameras. I'm the only muzungu in my remote village and even though I've been living here for about 10 months, I'm still a source of fascination; everything I do is observed. People gaze in wonderment as I buy laundry soap, purchase bananas, wash my coffee pot, eat chapatis. It's a good approximation, I suppose, of what people living in African villages must experience as foreigners troop through, staring unrelentingly and compulsively photographing them.

Uganda is not a camera culture, especially upcountry where I live. In the more distant villages people are not yet habituated to being photographed, and most of them have never taken a photograph themselves. Few have ever held a camera. They may have some photos of family members (which are proudly brought out when you visit people in their homes), but it's more likely you'll see only pictures of the Obusinga, the Rwenzori king, and President Museveni displayed in houses and shops around here.

Six days a week, I commute to my office on foot through a maze of trails that lead into people's yards, over fields, past a cassava mill and a brick kiln, and around various goats, chickens, pigs, cows and a band of marauding, knee-hugging toddlers. I carry my camera with me wherever I go, but I rarely remove it from my bag. It's odd, as this is one of the most photogenic places I've ever been, and it's populated with some of the most attractive people I've ever laid eyes on. Plus, most of them have a fashion sense that makes the work of the major designers look meek, lame and chromatically tepid.

My accidental no pictures policy is stranger still given that looking at photographs, and taking them, has been extremely important to me for more than four-and-a-half decades. Curiously, I have an enormous desire to take photographs, but I'm finding not doing so deeply satisfying. It's a conundrum, because in addition to having a powerful affinity for the creative act of making pictures, I find the act itself meditative and calming, and yet, I'm torn, because in this context there's also something off-putting about it.

Here's Susan Sontag's take on the subject in her 1977 book, "On Photography": "The very activity of taking pictures is soothing, and assuages general feelings of disorientation that are likely to be exacerbated by travel. Most tourists feel compelled to put the camera between themselves and whatever is remarkable that they encounter. Unsure of other responses, they take a picture. This gives shape to experience: stop, take a photograph, and move on. The method especially appeals to people handicapped by a ruthless work ethic — Germans, Japanese, and Americans. Using a camera appeases the anxiety which the work-driven feel about not working when they are on vacation and supposed to be having fun. They have something to do that is like a friendly imitation of work: they can take pictures."

Elsewhere in the book, Sontag says that the increasing ubiquity of photographs and cameras is causing people to develop a "chronic voyeuristic relation" to all that they behold (and she was writing long before the epidemic proliferation of cellphone cameras, and the easy, rapid multiplication and distribution of digital images). My rationale for not taking photographs in my village is simpler: I don't want to be the guy who's always walking around taking pictures of people. It's invasive, it's bad manners and it creates distance instead of camaraderie. It immediately defines you as other — you are the observer, your subject is the observed. You control the expensive machine; they don't. You decide when to shoot; they submit -- willingly or unwillingly. Also, it's a choice made by one person that instantly transforms everyone's experience of what is occurring at that moment.

Much as I love the making of pictures, for me, at this juncture in life, it's more important to experience than to record. Besides, does the world need one more photo of an African woman with firewood on her back, a lion and its cubs, raggedy village children, or a lounging gorilla dining on leaves? (I can't answer that question. Those are all pictures I've taken in the last few months.)

Even people in the remote villages may take exception to having their picture taken, be angered by it. Occasionally, it has to do with superstition, but I've found it also has to do with the widespread, often intuitive grasp of how Africa and Africans have been treated by outsiders -- for centuries. Foreigners have come in, paid little or nothing for Africa's abundant raw materials, taken them off the continent, and gotten rich. There is a deep understanding of that chain of events even among the illiterate. And some here see muzungus taking pictures as just one more form of colonialism, one more way of taking Africa's raw materials — in this case, its visual splendor — and turning them into something of value that has no benefit to Africans. It's the new digital colonialism.

The other side of that is that many here, especially children, love having their photo taken and will request it. The nice thing about digital cameras is that their big viewing screens make it possible to show the picture to the subject immediately. No matter what I'm photographing, I show the results to whoever happens to be nearby. That easy act is always appreciated, usually causes much laughter, and serves to remove the distance that pointing a camera at someone creates. And it satisfies the boundless curiosity about what the hell I'm up to.

This idea of the tyranny of photography, the almost uncontrollable compulsion to photograph that afflicts some of us when confronted with the strange and wonderful — rather than simply drinking in the experience we must stop it, freeze it, hold it forever as a thing, as a way of possessing it, owning it, keeping it, preventing the true ephemeral nature of the momentary event from escaping into the tunnel of time -- is a topic, perhaps an array of topics, I've had on my mind for some time. Coincidentally, in June, Seth Mydans wrote a piece about it in the New York Times' excellent "Lens" blog. The article was called "Too Many Lenses, Too Few Eyes." (The title either consciously or unconsciously echoes the apropos lyric by the Police: "Too many cameras, not enough food.") In the article, Mydans writes, "For many travelers, the goal of tourism now seems as much to be recording the trip as living the experience. This impulse is neatly captured in a photograph by Lydie France of the European Pressphoto Agency that shows a crowd of people around the Mona Lisa, several of them holding up small cameras for snapshots. Why? Who needs a snapshot of the Mona Lisa? Why not just look and appreciate? The camera seems to form a barrier between the viewer and the experience."

When I was in Paris, far too long ago, I was lucky to be alone in the room with the Mona Lisa. There were no photographers in sight to intrude on my moments with Mona. But 10 minutes later I was climbing the steps between two of the floors of the Louvre, looking up as I ascended, and there, on the landing, were four people standing before the Venus de Milo, cameras raised to their faces, rabidly clicking away at what must be one of the most photographed statues on earth.

More recently, I had the privilege of a one-hour audience with a family of mountain gorillas in Uganda's Bwindi Impenetrable Forest. I'd decided ahead of time not to take pictures. I didn't want to spend even a few fractions of those 60 minutes holding a camera between me and our luxuriantly shaggy, seriously laid-back, nearly extinct relatives. (Besides, I reasoned, the mountain gorillas photography group on Flickr has 227 members and who knows how many thousands of photos.)

It was a good decision. Too bad I didn't stick with it. Once I was among them, just having them near was adequately powerful to indelibly carve into my memory their faces and eyes and hands and hair and arms and legs and every gesture and glance. And yet, and yet ... it wasn't enough. As I stood within a few meters of one of the females and she looked over at me, my Dr. Strangelove hand found its way to the camera, turned it on, raised it to my face, gently

pressed the shutter button and click -- stopped time, locked it up in ones and zeros, briefly, surely, decisively removed me from it, and from directly experiencing that unrepeatable moment.

8 AUGUIST 2010

Sylvia's Wedding

Sylvia got married yesterday. She married David. She's lived next door to me ever since I arrived here; we also work for the same coffee cooperative. I don't recall ever seeing David, but when I showed up at the Catholic church yesterday morning, there he was holding Sylvia's hand as the priest announced them man and wife. Sylvia looked like a queen, but then she always does; she's gorgeous. David looked very happy, which was totally understandable. And he seems to adore her, which proves he's in his right mind.

Sylvia is a rascal. One day, during the first week or two I was living in the village, I met her as I was walking home. I was carrying a bunch of sweet bananas. "Oh," she said, "what nice bananas!" And she quickly broke off two of them and scampered away. Ever since that episode we've had a running joke in which I make a big show of hiding any bananas I'm carrying when I see her. And if I'm going away overnight and have some bananas in the house, I give them to Sylvia and she reacts as if I've just handed her the Hope Diamond. It is all quite silly and endlessly entertaining.

There was a couple of hours break after the wedding, and then the reception kicked off at David's parents' house, across the river and up the hill through the matooke groves past Teddy's place. It was the usual modest Ugandan wedding party — about 500 extravagantly dressed people, several large herds of children, umpteen babies, a deafening sound system, a shouting DJ whose nonstop patter was totally indecipherable except for every 10th word, which was either "Sylvia!" or "David!" and a half-dozen cakes. And fireworks. It resembled a psychedelic African coronation with a single lone muzungu in attendance. The addled ambassador from Outer Muzunguland.

Sylvia fed David cake, and David fed Sylvia cake. Sylvia brought a big plate of cake to David's mother, and then the gift giving started. The bride and groom, a bit spaced-out and exhausted-looking by that time, stood behind a table as people came up in twos and threes and delivered gift-wrapped boxes, a chicken, a goat and a 20-gallon jerri can of palm oil. (Sylvia once made me Nile perch fried in palm oil and it was so good I almost cried.)

Once all the presents were received and admired, it was time for photos. One woman took it upon herself to pose the bride and groom. First she had Sylvia stand behind David on a stool and sling her arm over his shoulder, so it looked like he was carrying his new wife caveman style. Then David stood behind Sylvia on the stool and slung his arm over her shoulder, so it looked like she was carrying her new husband cavewoman style. The posing continued in that vein for a very long time, David and Sylvia following the woman's increasingly insane directions with endless patience and good nature even though the afternoon heat was merciless.

I decided to leave about then, though the party went on into the evening. Once at home, I lay on my bed and let the local dog choir serenade me, and thought about whether David and Sylvia will go the distance. I think they will. If they could make it through that photo session, they can make it through anything.

11 AUGUST 2010

It's Only Rock in Road, II: The Burning Boulder

Faithful readers will recall the earlier piece about the gigantic rock in the middle of the road in my village. After several days of digging around the iceberg-like monolith, and with its base nowhere in sight, I think despair set in among the road crew. They walked away from it, let the goats take it over as a sleeping platform, and continued working elsewhere on the road. Several days later, the entire road was essentially finished, but the rock was still sitting there like a great pimple, a goat-covered pimple. Apparently news of the immovable blemish finally reached the head office and early this week two young guys who looked to have more enthusiasm than skill were sent out to do battle with it.

They came equipped with sledges and wedges and massive iron breaker bars 6 feet long. One of them wore a bandanna printed with an attractive marijuana motif. They were all hopped up with determination. But their weapons of choice turned out to be old, dry tree stumps. Somewhere they'd collected about six or eight of them, their scraggly roots still attached. Our two heroes arranged the stumps to completely cover the rock, like a great toupee, then doused the whole thing in way too many jerri cans full of kerosene, which is called paraffin here.

Before they lit it, I took a picture and the twosome then demanded I buy them a soda. "You buy me a soda," I said. "I took the picture. I didn't even want a picture of you. I was trying to take a picture of the rock and you got in the way. You oughta buy me two sodas and a chapati, and two skewers of muchomo!" (Muchomo is grilled goat meat.)

The cannier of the two saw that a new strategy was called for and rapidly recalibrated his approach. "Let's be friends," he said, and extended his hand. That made me feel about 2 feet tall. I shook his hand and we vowed to be best friends forever and ever. Then I walked over to a nearby store, bought them each a soda, and walked back to the rock.

A large crowd had gathered because who doesn't like watching something burst into flame? The crowd was not disappointed. In fact, it was nearly ignited. As soon as the first match was tossed on the paraffin-soaked roots, a humongous fireball enveloped the stump-rock construction. It was as if Andy Goldsworthy had been asked to remake "Towering Inferno." We were all knocked back about 10 feet by the heat wall, and several goats took off toward the river like racehorses. Once the conflagration calmed down, it became clear that the project was going to be an all-day sucker, so I continued up to my office. I harbored grave doubts about the likelihood of the two soda sippers achieving anything, but on my way home I was surprised to find they'd succeeded.

The immense heat enabled by their over-zealous application of paraffin had shattered the rock and they were busy pulling the colossus apart and tossing the chunks to the side of the road. Within a couple of hours, the thing was mostly gone and the hole was filled with dirt and smoothed over. The next morning, boda-boda drivers were madly racing up and down the road while several goats gazed wistfully at the spot where their conveniently located sleeping platform had once been.

17 AUGUST 2010

Darkness in Daytime

Noisy crowds often gather in the village — to hear politicians, or buy fresh fish, or watch a card game, or register to vote. But today's crowd wasn't one of those. It was silent. No one spoke except in the softest whisper. They were all gazing at a white Toyota sedan slowly driving toward the bridge, which leads to the road that goes to the hospital. Around noon, just up the path from my office, a 7-year-old boy had slipped from a tree while chopping a high branch. He was killed by the fall.

Gathering firewood is a never-ending pursuit in Uganda. All the cooking fires are fueled with wood or charcoal, and virtually all cooking is done over flames. The country is losing its forests at a ferocious rate. Much of the easy-to-get wood is gone, so people — mainly women and children — walk farther, go up and down long, steep hills, climb tall trees to collect enough branches and twigs to cook the night's meal.

There are deaths in the village every week, usually old people, sometimes babies; typically because of illness, occasionally due to accidents. Perhaps it's the very frequency and familiarity of death, its closeness and non-negotiable, arbitrary nature, that gives this culture its penchant for joy and joking, its sense of fun and quick embrace of good times. As I often tell friends in the U.S., carpe diem is official policy here.

But for a while today's tragedy froze the village, and even now, as I write this, several hours since the child's fall, the usual market-day noises seem muffled and distant, I hear no babies crying, no dogs barking, and the generator at the cassava mill is shut down. The boda-boda drivers are no longer raucously zooming about, and the gray of the sky looks like it will never leave.

10 SEPTEMBER 2010

The Lost

As crazy as Kampala is, you only rarely see crazy walking the streets. I suspect real crazy doesn't survive for long here outside of an institution. I have seen a couple of small mental hospitals while traveling the country. They appeared to be as appealing as mental hospitals anywhere, and the patients looked reasonably well cared for. In the year I've been in Uganda I've come across maybe a half-dozen people on the street who were obviously wrestling with psychosis and losing the match to the Big Dog of Darkness. If insanity is widespread here, I've seen little evidence of it on the sidewalks and pathways, in the parks and doorways; it's certainly not as ubiquitous among those living on the ragged edge in this country as it is among their counterparts in San Francisco, L.A. or Manhattan.

Madness, the heart-eating, soul-twisting, mind-warping, hallucinatory variety, has stormed past my life on numerous occasions since I was a child. You'd think I'd be able to spot it pretty quickly by now, even at a distance. It's easy enough here in the village where we have a single mildly crazy soul whom I encounter once or twice a week. He mutters and smiles and argues with himself, dresses in filthy rags and carries a large club with him wherever he goes. The club is a tree branch he has meticulously wrapped in strips of black rubber inner tube. It looks like something out of a New Yorker caveman cartoon. He doesn't do anything with the club. He's not aggressive. He just lugs it around.

The other night I was at the Ndere Center in Kampala. It's an open air theater that offers a program of tribal dancing and music three nights a week. It's a terrific way to sample the richness of African culture. And dinner and drinks are served during the performances.

About 7 p.m., just before the show begins with an Acholi courting dance, I'm up getting a plate of food. About 30 yards away is our table. We've left our two Nile Lagers sitting on it while we retrieve our meals. I watch as a young woman of 20 or so sits down next to our places. No problem — that's the setup: Several people share a table. You may know them, you may not. She seems to be alone. She glances around, removes her jacket and puts it on the back of her chair, brushes back her hair, turns to her left, grabs my beer, takes a big chug and puts it back on the table.

I didn't quite believe I'd seen it, so I continued to watch her. She did it a second time and a third. I left my food with the chef and walked briskly over to her. She saw me approaching, took another gulp of the Nile. I stopped in front of her.

"Why are you drinking my beer?"

"S-sorry ... I didn't mean to. I thought it was mine."

I was just about to get seriously pissed off when I noticed the deep, dark sorrow in her brown eyes. She was lost and empty and scared. And she was so upset, so authentically contrite, and so clearly out of her mind. Who knows what she was doing there, but once I understood that something heartbreaking had ahold of her, I did my best to gracefully retreat.

"My mistake," I said. "I think it is yours."

"That's OK, sir," she said, and took another swig.

I walked back to get my food, and then we found another table. About halfway through the performance, I glanced back at her. She was ignoring the dancers, smiling broadly and carefully, thoroughly peeling the label off of the Nile bottle.

14 SEPTEMBER 2010

Enos Crosses Over

One morning during the first week I was living in the village, Enos walked across the road from his carpentry shop to my office and introduced himself. We chatted aimlessly for a while, then he stood up to leave. "And you will come to dinner at my home," he said. "My wife will cook goat and obundu, we'll drink beer. But next Saturday, come to the shop and meet some of my students. They'll tell their stories."

On Saturday morning I walked up to Enos' workshop. For several years he'd been training orphans, older teenagers mostly, in carpentry and tailoring. He'd gathered about eight of them to talk with me, males and females. They sat in a semicircle around me and, one by one, told me of their lives. One boy had lost both his grandfather and his father when the ADF rebels from the Democratic Republic Congo had come through this village during the 1997-2003 war. A girl of about 20, who had made the splendid batengi fabric outfit she was wearing, was raising her three younger siblings; both their parents had died of AIDS. It went on like that — one harrowing account after another — until it was my turn to talk. I had little to say and it took me a long time to say it: "Wasinkya kutsibu for telling me your stories. I'm sorry you've had so much sorrow in your short lives. And I'm proud of you for doing the things you're doing now so you can get good jobs." That was the best I could do.

"Wasinkya erisima," several of them said. That means "Thank you for appreciating."

In the months after that, as I walked to and from work every day, I'd stop by Enos' shop for a short visit. We continued to get to know each other. Sometimes I'd have him and his students build furniture for my house — a bed, a table, a picnic table for the courtyard. He also made all the desks for the local primary school and benches for the churches. Just a couple weeks ago he came by my office with an unexpected gift: a laminated wood serving tray he'd made me. "For you," was all he said, and turned his palms to me to gesture "no payment."

I was away in Kampala for two weeks and returned last Friday afternoon. On Saturday morning, Enos came over to my office and sat down. I told him about what I'd done in Kampala. He told me about what had been going on in the village. He was wearing what's lately seemed to be his favorite outfit: a blinding red sweat suit. I said he looked good and asked how he was feeling. "I feel fine," he said. We agreed he'd take me down to the tailoring shop in a few days so I could have a couple of shirts made, and he suggested I come over for dinner again sometime soon.

On Sunday, Asaba, who rarely calls me, phoned while I was cleaning the house. "Mr. Doug-a-las," she said in her beautiful, buttery accent. "Ms. Asaba!" I responded, making fun of her formality as I always do. But this time she didn't laugh as she always does. "Mr. Doug-a-las, Enos has died." We said a few other things as we stumbled to "Goodbye." Enos had gone to church, Asaba told me. He led the singing (he was a gifted musician and composer in addition to being a master carpenter), then asked to be taken to Kagando Hospital where he died, apparently of kidney failure. He was in his 30s, with a wife and young child.

Sunday afternoon Enos' body was brought from the hospital to his home here in the village. At about 5 p.m. Esther and I walked over, made our way through the yard that was packed with people, many of whom were sobbing and wailing, and into the small main room of Enos' house. I'd been in that room before in the near darkness, eating goat and obundu by the light of a kerosene lamp and drinking warm Nile Lager, while Enos showed me a photo album of his family. On Sunday the room was warm and humid from all the people crowded into it. Enos lay on his back on the bed, wrapped in a red, floral-printed Chinese blanket. There was a small piece of cotton in each of his nostrils. Esther and I stood and looked at Enos, nodded to some of the people we knew, and then departed.

A month or so ago, Enos had asked me if I'd walk up to his mother's house with him. She lives on top of a small hill overlooking the village and he was thinking of building a bed and breakfast there; he wanted my opinion of the location. It was just the two of us. His mother was away. We talked about how to position the buildings, how the rooms' decks should look out at the view of the village, and if the climb up the hill would be a problem for some guests. I took a picture of him in front of his mother's house. He was standing at the side of the neatly swept dirt courtyard. He was wearing his red sweat suit.

The next time I was in that yard was yesterday — for Enos' funeral and burial. To get there we walked across the village, through the banana groves, and over the creaky rough-cut plank bridge that I photographed Enos crossing a few weeks ago. Many people were walking with us, and hundreds were on the hill and in the yard of the house. Enos' brother Eric saw us and helped us through the crowd. He took us to a bench near the front of the seating, about 10 feet from the coffin, which was covered with a blue fabric that had a large white cross stitched onto it. The box had a small window through which Enos' face could be seen, though from where I was sitting I could only see his graceful, prominent nose. I could also tell that the Chinese blanket was still wrapped around him.

It was hot and crowded and the plastic tarp that had been rigged on sapling trunks to provide shade made it hotter. There was singing of hymns and prayer and more singing. At one point two women carried Enos' wife out of the house. She was crying loudly and couldn't walk on her own. She slumped on the ground next to the coffin near Enos' mother who was also crying. There were at least half a dozen preachers, representing every denomination with a church in the village, and representing every church that Enos had built benches for.

There were many speeches, all in Lhukonzo, by friends and local officials, and then the tallest of the preachers stood up, a man with a classic, deep, sermon-delivering voice. He spoke in Lhukonzo so I caught little of what he said, but every once in a while he'd throw in an English phrase: "Let me go prepare a place for you." He repeated it rhythmically, weaving it in and out of the Lhukonzo. "Let me go prepare a place for you." Sometimes whispering, sometimes shouting. "Let me go prepare a place for you." He'd say things that people would laugh at wildly, and other things they'd applaud. "Let me go prepare a place for you," he said again as he motioned with his hands for everyone to stand and for the pallbearers to pick up the casket. "Let me go prepare a place for you," he said one last time and all of us moved to the yard where the grave had been dug; we'd heard them digging during the service.

Once we got to the grave site, a few more words were said, another hymn was sung, and the preacher nodded to the pallbearers. They passed ropes to one another under the coffin, and slowly lowered it.

11 OCTOBER 2010

Second Floor Balcony: The Movie

The balcony of the White House Hotel is perfect. Or maybe not. Or perhaps it is perfect in its imperfection. I suppose it is not the most perfect place on the planet, not in any conventional sense. It's not the terrace of a glorious hotel in Venice or Paris or Tahiti. It's not even attached to one of the more extravagant inns in Uganda, like the Emin Pasha in Kampala or Ndali Lodge near Kibale Forest. And the hotel itself has no infinity pool, no pool at all. It has a small upstairs cafe with white plastic tables covered by lemon yellow Bell Lager tablecloths, and next to the cafe, a lounge with a couple of couches and a flat-screen TV that shows Sky News, CNN or football — as in Arsenal vs. Manchester United — at high volume. There is also a table with fake flowers and a stuffed toy tiger.

Located about an hour from my home, I stay at the White House two or three times a month when I need to be in hot, dusty, valley-floor Kasese for more than a day, or if I just require a break from the hectic pace of a small African village high in the Rwenzori Mountains.

Florence, the manager, seems to take pleasure in giving me the same room — No. 4 — if it's available, as if I had my honeymoon there or signed landmark legislation under its ka-chunking fan, the same one that chopped the tendon of my right middle finger about a month ago.

After I dump my stuff on the bed and take my first hot shower in a couple of weeks, I walk across the inner courtyard of the building, through the cafe and out to the second-floor balcony. If there are no chairs, someone brings one for me, and Annette or Jimmy carries out a small knee-high table and sets it to the side of the chair. I greet them in Lhukonzo and they laugh at my pathetic pronunciation. "Usual, Doug-a-las?" Jimmy or Annette will then ask. "Usual," I say.

Really now, you can't put a price on having a place, especially a small upstairs place in a little hotel in a dusty town in western Uganda, where they know you by name and actually ask if you want your "usual." From what 1940s movie did this place emerge? All that's missing is Peter Lorre lurking about in the background and Sidney Greenstreet wearing a dirty linen suit, stinking of gin, and slumped over at a corner table with a hyacinth macaw on his shoulder.

A few minutes after I'm visited by Annette or Jimmy on the balcony, an impossibly cold Eagle Lager descends to the knee-high table. I hand back the glass, which I never use but they always bring, and gaze southwest, to the setting sun and the clouds rolling over the mountains like tumbleweeds made of froth.

Below, on the brick patio at the entry of the hotel, a few people are seated under a vine-covered arbor. Sometimes I overhear the whispers of lovers. Other times it's the inebriated bellows of the local politicians. Beyond them is a big orange dirt lot that separates the hotel from the macadam road, which leads up to the old copper mining town of Kilembe. But it's not really a dirt lot. It's a movie screen, and it's the thing that makes the second floor balcony of the White House Hotel one of the planet's perfect places.

As the setting sun washes the sky and the mountains with light the color of ripe cantaloupe, I watch the dirt lot. Across it pass groups of Muslim schoolgirls (bright pink outfits, white head scarves); men pushing bicycles loaded with bunches of matooke; women carrying trussed-up chickens and tugging at goats; teenage boys selling tawdry newspapers, oily samosas and hot chapatis; businessmen, nuns, soldiers, drunks, children, grandfathers, grandmothers, cripples, cows, singers, arguers, marabou storks and muzungus like me, who are coming to the White House Hotel to sit on the second-floor balcony, have a couple of Eagle Lagers and watch the floorshow as the sky slips through lavender into blackness, a blackness violently splashed with the Milky Way.

19 OCTOBER 2010

The Listening Tour

If we more or less agree on evolution theory, Africa is not only where it all began for humans, it's the most likely birthplace of music. It makes sense, then, that the people who have been playing music the longest are the best at it.

African music is extraordinarily varied, lively, rich and utterly intoxicating. Fortunately, there is plenty of it. And you don't have to find it, it finds you. There is an abundance of traditional music everywhere you turn here, but also the contemporary music industry in Africa is hyper-productive.

Despite what seems a never-ending tragedy in the D.R. Congo, the music that comes out of that country is exquisite, such as the songs of the fine, jazzy balladeer Franco, who died in 1989, though his work is still extremely popular. While Senegal, Mali, Nigeria, Benin and other West Africa nations have produced numerous artists who have been, and continue to be, enormously influential, including the incandescent Angelique Kidjo from Benin, and the late Ali Farka Touré (and now his son, Vieux Farka Touré) from Mali, who played in a style that Martin Scorsese aptly called "the DNA of the blues."

And then there are scores of strong Ugandan Afro-pop stars like Jose Chameleone, Bebe Cool, Bobbi Wine, Michael Ross Kakooza, Radio & Weasel, Aziz Azion, and Juliana Kanyomozi (whom I met at a hotel in Mbarara a few months ago; she was singing at a wedding, and she is a tall drink of water).

And when music from other parts of the world comes here, it is given the indelible stamp of Africanness. Throughout the week, there are choir practices at the Anglican Church just across the road from my office. The sweet sound of hymns being sung in Lhukonzo softens my suffering in luscious, Bantu-inflected fashion while I'm plodding through a spreadsheet or drafting a concept paper. On Sundays, to begin services and end them, men drum outside the chapel. At wedding receptions, which I seem to go to about once a month lately, there is plenty of impromptu singing, though it often gets drowned out by the Richter scale-shattering thrump of the sound systems and the screaming MCs.

But I do my most concentrated, focused listening in private-hire cars on the several-hour-long drives I make across Uganda every few weeks. Sometimes it's just the two-hour cruise up to Fort Portal, lifting from the valley floor into the high, green tea country before rolling into what is — both literally and figuratively — one of Uganda's coolest towns. And there are times I must go to Kampala. That's a six-hour trip, sometimes more.

After enduring a dozen or so long, sweaty, crowded, grumpiness-generating marathons on the big, bumpy bus back and forth between here and Kampala, it occurred to me that one of the benefits of having been in the workforce for 40 years before taking this assignment is that I've got a little more scratch than my much younger fellow Americans, and can thus afford to avoid some of the less appealing aspects of this experience, such as long, sweaty, crowded, grumpiness-generating marathons on the big, bumpy bus back and forth between here and Kampala. So I now indulge in private-hire cars for long road trips. It also gets me a superior audio experience and has vastly enlarged my music collection, and added to my circle of friends.

By now, I have assembled a cadre of favorite drivers, all of whom arrive on time, charge a reasonable rate, pilot cars that don't strand us, and are entertaining conversationalists, or skilled non-talkers when the mood is a contemplative one. They also suggest great cafes down side streets in small towns, know where the ATMs are in every village along our route, and have the rockin'est music on the road. In Kampala I use Farouk. If he's not available, I get Steve Taxi, Angela or Geoffrey. In Fort Portal and all around the western part of the country, I hire Saturday, Julius, sometimes Adolf. And my all-time favorite is still Moses the Intrepid, my organization's staff driver.

All of them have those small MP3 players that plug into the car's cigarette lighter and, thanks to some kind of big magic, play through the vehicle's audio system. The music itself resides on a USB flash drive. Some drivers have four or five 8-gigabyte flashes — hundreds and hundreds of songs: great stuff out of Congo, Uganda, Nigeria, Tanzania, slick pop from South Africa, and the odd schmaltzy radio hit from America, like "Lady in Red."

I'd been going on splendid music-infused car trips for months before my wee brain had a large realization. It took me a while to make that breakthrough, but I've lost no time since. I now have folders on my computer of "Joshua's Driving Music," "Moses' Driving Music," "Saturday's Driving Music" and so on. I play it throughout the day; people frequently come into my office and dance. It happened just a few minutes ago when Victoria was walking through the yard to pick some basil out of my garden and chase away a couple of goats that will not leave the maize alone. I'm working on a mind-bending budget for a grant, so I've got the music blasting. Just as Victoria passed my door, "Nkyali Bubi," a terrific song by Ugandan artists Diamond Oscar and GNL Zamba, started playing and Victoria began bobbing her head and funkily throwing her feet around, rhythmically kicking at the freshly cut grass. "Dougalasee," she yelled to me, "look, I'm dancing!"

Then there was the time Joshua and I were driving to Mbarara, about two hours from here, and a song I really liked was playing. I'd never heard it before. It had a great sound with a complex rhythm structure — wicked good beats all over the place — and the sensual, bawdy lyrics sung by a woman with a lush, tough voice were, um, attention-getting and unencumbered by euphemism: "I like the way you touch me there. I like the way you pull my hair."

"Whoa!" I said to Joshua. "Where is this song from? Is it Ugandan? It's not Congolese is it?"

"No," Joshua replied. "That's from the USA. It's 'Rude Boy' by Rihanna."

26 OCTOBER 2010

Home

I have lived in this village for a year, a year and eight days. I'll be here for another year, maybe more. I stay in a small compound of one- and two-room accommodations on the village's southern edge, surrounded by banana groves, near the river and the market. The front of the building is the coffee warehouse for the cooperative that employs me. To enter my home, I walk through the warehouse or around the side of the building and into the courtyard.

There is no ornamentation in the courtyard, just grey cement walls, blue doors and shutters. Before my friend Enos died, I had him build a picnic table and benches so people have a place to sit outside. My neighbors use it day and night. It's very satisfying to see them sitting in the darkness, illuminated by a kerosene lamp, cutting up fish or reading or drinking tea — and looking like a painting of 21st-century Africans by Vermeer. Sometimes I join them. Sometimes I don't.

One of the things I like about this home is that even when I choose to spend a day or evening alone, flopped on my bed reading, texting, writing email, I hear my neighbors, their children and the life of the village beyond. When the wind comes up, signaling the approach of rain, the banana trees that hang over the tin roof rattle and scrape. Occasionally one of the panda-patterned crows swoops through the courtyard, its barking voice echoing off the walls. On hot, clear, moony nights, bats zip about spasmodically, beeping along with the cellphones that light up every hand.

The place is two rooms, roughly the size of the kitchen in my former home in the United States. Across the courtyard is a shower and toilet that I share with my neighbors. There is a water spigot that works for a day or two, stops, flows again, stops and so on. When it's been off for a few days then starts, everyone rushes out with their jerri cans and fills them. I keep three 20-gallon ones: One for cooking water; two others for drinking water, which I treat with purifier. It's probably not necessary to purify the water. There's not much between this village and the glacier that feeds the river. But I do anyway. I brought very little with me and I haven't acquired much while I've been here — some books, a couple of shirts, plastic dishes, a two-burner hot plate, kerosene lamps, batengi fabric and a couple of thin plaid blankets that came out of Kenya where they are favored by the Masai who wear them as shawls.

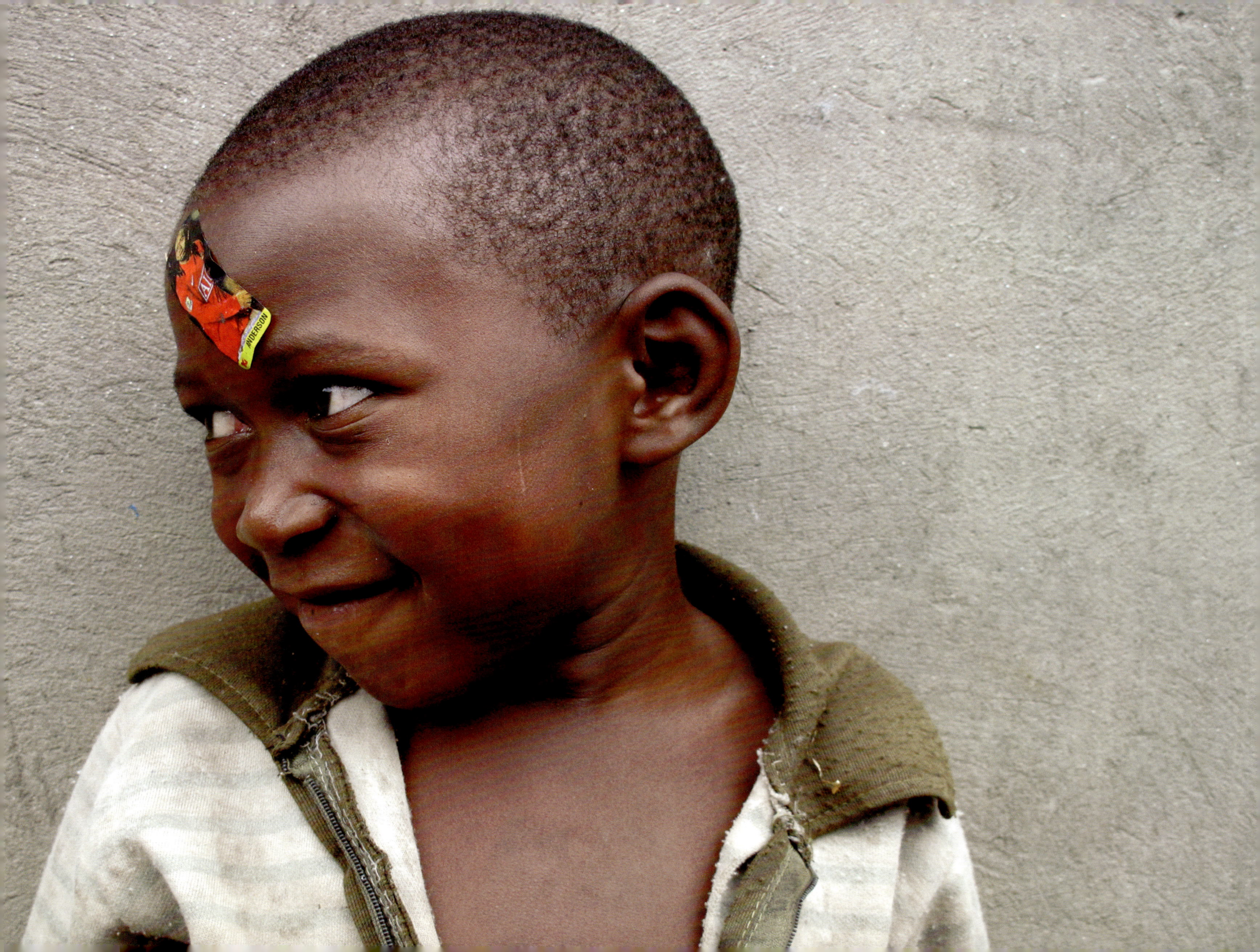

4 NOVEMBER 2010

Some Kind of Son

Part of my morning getting-ready-for-work ritual is standing in the outside doorway to my rooms, holding a hand mirror while I shave with my Gillette Mach 3. Ten feet away stands Ronaldo, 5 years old, with a small piece of cardboard or a stick, mimicking every stroke I make with the razor. He duplicates my movements exactly. He's one of the most observant children I've ever met.

He homed in on me earlier this year and became something of a shadow, and I took a liking to him too. At first he chattered away at me in his own brand of Lhukonzo, but now he speaks a few sentences of English, and I reciprocate by speaking a little Lhukonzo to him. And we use sign language.

Most mornings, after I shave, I make Ronaldo a chapati slathered with crunchy peanut butter and marmalade, I fill the light green plastic cup with water, and I sit him down at the outside table. While he chews away at breakfast and drips peanut butter and marmalade all over the table, I do the previous night's dishes, brush my teeth, take the laundry off the line. At some point I ask him if the chapati is good and he gives me two thumbs up, just like a small, African Roger Ebert. After he's finished eating, Ronaldo washes the cup and brings it to my door. He never enters unless invited.

Later in the day, he'll often show up at my office. I frequently play music while I'm working and Ronaldo likes to stand by my desk and dance. Occasionally I'll dance with him without leaving my chair. On Monday, the two of us were flailing away to Aziz Azion's "Yegwe" and in walked Father Simon, the young Catholic priest from the church up the road. He bopped along with us for a couple of minutes.

What's best is when Ronaldo comes by on a Sunday when I'm reading or using the computer, and slowly, meticulously scans every shelf and table. Sometimes he'll take five minutes or more, standing in the same spot, looking, and then point at something: a book, a jar, a box, a map. I'll hand it to him and he'll slowly open or unfold it, like an archaeologist examining a new find. He takes his time, scrutinizes it very closely. Ronaldo likes pictures of animals; he often asks for the birds of Uganda book. (I once asked him which bird looked like me and he pointed to a spoonbill stork, not the handsomest of creatures. I took the book away from him.) The other day it was a pair of broken eyeglasses that fascinated him. He spent much of an hour with those damaged spectacles.

He picks up on my moods quickly. If I'm in a funk, he stays nearby, but doesn't intrude. And he never has to be told anything twice. One day I was semi-napping, meditating, ruminating, cogitating about the changes of the last year, how the other shore has receded, causing some people to drift closer and others to fade away. I was vaguely wondering what and where I'll return to, and how I'd say goodbye to the people who are now in my life — such as Ronaldo. The window shutters were open, but the curtain was drawn, trembling in the afternoon breeze. Ronaldo drew it back from outside and peered in at me. I was annoyed.

"Don't do that, Ronaldo," I snapped at him, and he quickly disappeared.

Then I felt bad about scolding him for simply being curious. After all, he didn't know what rules of privacy and protocol I'd established. In fact, like most of the children here, he's impeccably polite. Well, I thought, I'll give him something else to look through, something other than my window. So, as I had several months ago with Madeline, I gave him a kaleidoscope. It was the last one left from the six or eight I brought with me.

That night, after getting up from my nap, I found Ronaldo out in the courtyard. I handed him a hard-boiled egg and kept one for myself. We sat outside dipping our eggs into a bowl of salt, taking a bite, dipping again. He got a bunch of pieces of yolk in the salt, but I didn't care.

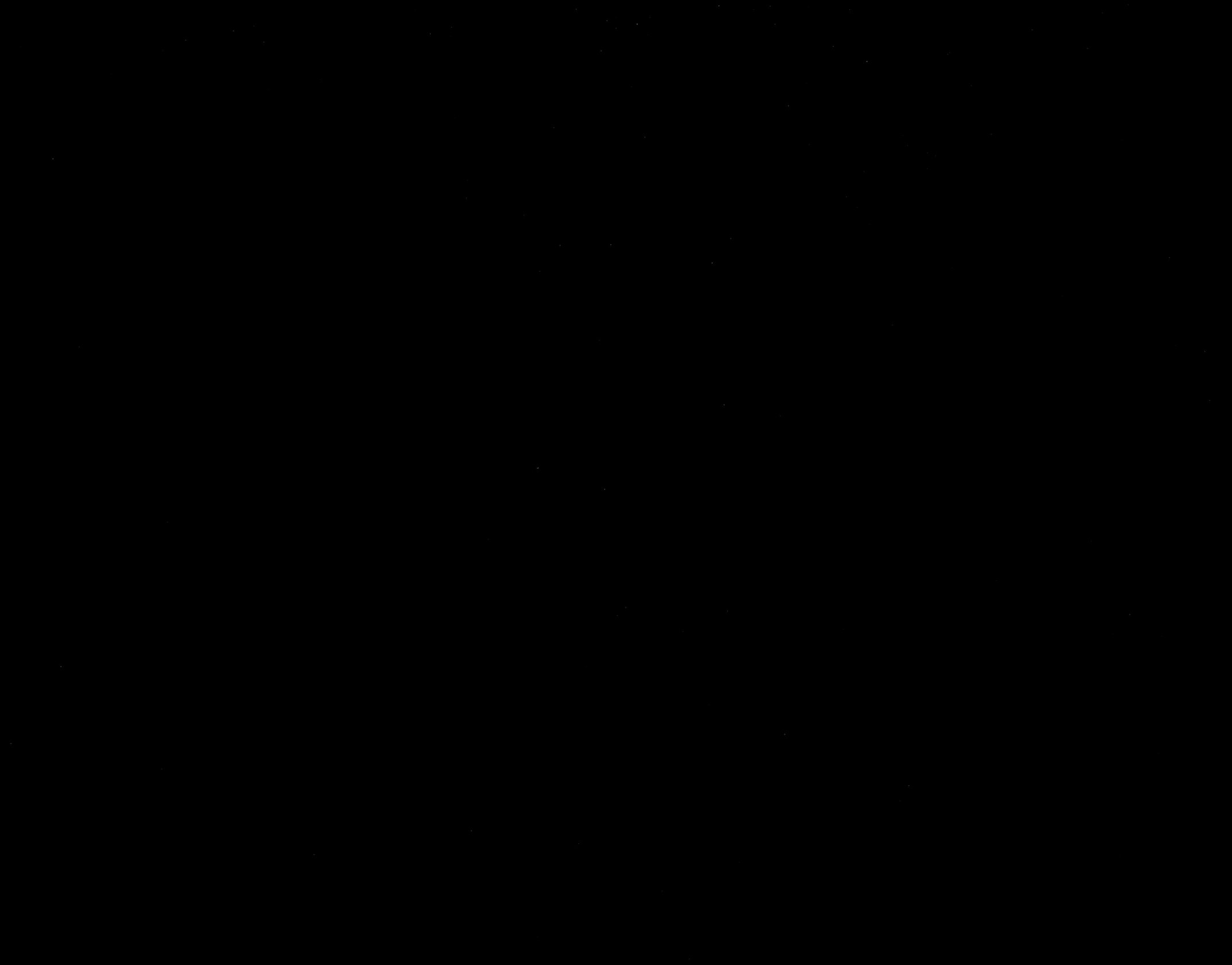

5 NOVEMBER 2010

Portrait of the Author as a Driven Man

A couple of weeks ago, a driver I frequently use, named Saturday, pulled up in front of my hotel in Fort Portal, jumped out of the car and ran back to the trunk. He was in a state of high excitement, not a typical condition for Saturday as he tends to be a cool, calm character.

"I have something for you," he said. "A surprise." He could not stand still. He was downright giddy.

Saturday opened the trunk and with a great flourish pulled out a canvas, flipped it over and there we were, the two of us, standing on the shore of Lake Bunyoni in Southwest Uganda. I'd given him a photograph taken of us when we were there last May, and he'd provided it to an artist to render in oil paint on a 2½-foot canvas. I hugged him, thanked him lavishly and off we drove. It now hangs in my rooms, gazing at me insistently.

The picture itself is all one could hope for. I like that the artist, whose name, unfortunately, I don't know, chose to leave Saturday's ever-present earphones for his mobile in place. And my maniacal gaze, which makes me look even more off-kilter than I actually am, gives the picture an air of menace and dramatic tension that it wouldn't otherwise have. But the painter's long suit is clearly landscape, as he or she has enthusiastically imposed a deliciously spooky, sensuous array of flora onto the shores of Lake Bunyoni that I don't recall being there — there are some trees, but none as animated and eerie as the ones in the portrait.

If, however, in the case of the muzungu, it is more a psychological portrait in the spirit, if not the style, of, say, Lucian Freud or Francis Bacon, then the landscape is, perhaps, right on the money.

20 NOVEMBER 2010

Cloudless Day, Entebbe

Sunday was feet and hands day at the zoo. Also tusks. The largest ostrich I've ever seen had some wicked-strange clodhoppers. I haven't spent that much time looking at ostrich feet. I know they can do damage, but after studying this feathered brute's pups I have a more vivid picture.

At the other end of the extremities spectrum were the tiny, soft-as-silk hands of the monkey that slowly, meticulously groomed my friend Nattabi's fingertips, gently picking off any little bit of dead flesh, stroking a small scar on her knuckle and, finally — so taken was he with her chocolate sauce skin — trying to pull her into the cage with him. She visits that particular monkey every time she goes to the zoo, she tells me, and he always gives her cuticles a thorough grooming.

Visiting the zoo in Africa may seem a strange activity, but the one at Entebbe, situated on the shore of the ocean that is Lake Victoria, is an especially agreeable spot to fritter away an afternoon. All the animals — lions, rhinos, chimps and many others — are rescues, saved from the pits, snares and artillery of poachers. The place itself is on the wild side. You wander down long dirt paths thinking you're lost, come around a corner and there's a massive forest hog, with bristly black hair curling out of its ears and tusks spiraling out of its mouth, a giraffe galloping across a meadow, or a pond full of otters. ("That's my mother's clan," Nattabi says, "the Otter Clan!")

Entebbe is perhaps one of the few Uganda place names Americans recognize, thanks to the "Raid on Entebbe" movie and also the reenactment of the dark Amin-era episode in "The Last King of Scotland" (a film several people I know here appeared in, including my trenchantly funny British doctor). But Entebbe is the polar opposite of that lingering image. It is a lovely, pastoral area where families go to the beach (or the zoo) on Sundays, and tourists stay at lushly landscaped inns before catching their morning flights out to the First World.

In his monologue performance film "Swimming to Cambodia," Spalding Gray tells of a cloud, a black vaporous specter that orbits the globe, stopping to haunt and sew sorrow. It halts over a star-crossed land, drops its dark curtain, brings hell to earth. In recent decades it has parked over Cambodia, over Bosnia, over Rwanda, New York City and Uganda.

But then it leaves. It departed Uganda decades ago, and a day at the Entebbe zoo is as good a confirmation of that as one could hope for.

3 DECEMBER 2010

Stairway to Heaven

There are chartreuse grasshoppers everywhere as I make the long and winding hike up the great tower. They are flying and hopping and flopping and sometimes smashing into me, and dying on the concrete steps that spiral up the inside of the minaret that reaches high into the air above the Gadhafi National Mosque in Kampala.

It was completed in 2006 and financed, as you can guess, by Col. Moammar Gadhafi, the leader of Libya. It is the third-largest mosque in Africa (Nos. 1 and 2 are in Egypt and Morocco). I'd been told I wouldn't be able to go inside, but upon arrival in the parking lot I am enthusiastically greeted by rifle-hugging, camouflage-wearing police, given a guestbook to sign and directed to climb the steps to the mosque's massive front doors. On the way up the staircase, someone gently asks me to remove my sandals, which I do. Once inside, I ask the guard if it is OK to take photographs. He seems surprised at the question. "Of course," he says, "take all the pictures you like."

The vast white room is empty except for a small boy who wanders around some, gazes up at the chandeliers that were made in Egypt, and then kneels down to pray. Later he joins me, taking my hand for a while and laughing when I show him each photo after I take it.

At one point, the boy leads me over to the large Quran that Gadhafi gave to the mosque and stands next to it. I take his picture with the huge book then hold the camera out for him to see. He giggles loudly enough to make an echo. The guard scowls at us from across the room, and walks briskly to where we're standing.

I think he's going to scold us, but instead he affectionately rubs the boy on the head and takes his hand. "Let me show you the ladies' gallery," he says.

"Is he your son?" I ask as we walk.

"No, he's my brother's son, my nephew."

We go up to a mezzanine overlooking the main floor. The guard flips a wall switch and the chandeliers light up throughout the entire mosque.

"Wow," I say.

"Wow," the boy says.

"This place was designed by a very young man, a boy, really, a Libyan," the guard tells me. "He was paid much money by Gadhafi."

We walk down from the mezzanine and outside. I lean back and take a photo looking up at the tower.

"Can we go up in it?" I ask.

"No," the guard says. "It is much money to go up in."

"How much?"

"Ten thousand," he says solemnly. (That's about $5.)

"I'd pay ten thousand to go to the top." I hand him the purple shillings note.

"Fine," he says. "Webale, ssebo." He pulls a key from his pocket, walks to the door at the base of the tower, opens a padlock and we enter what resembles the interior of a chambered nautilus. And up we climb. And climb. And climb some more. I'm trudging and sweating; he's nearly galloping, not a bead of sweat on him.

He stops to wait for me on a landing and when I reach him he points at the floor littered with small, light green cadavers. "Do you see the grasshoppers? They are going to heaven."

At the top, the reward is immediate: I step out onto the terrace and there, in every direction, is a view of Kampala that's even better than Google Earth. Straight ahead, the old and new bus parks. To the right, the Kabaka's palace. And far, far below, in his new silver Toyota Ipsum, is my driver, Farouk. I wave for a long time but get no response.

When I get back to the Toyota, I tell Farouk I waved to him from the top of the tower. "I would have seen you, my brother" he says, "but I was napping. And I would have taken a picture — if I'd had a camera."

"Webale, ssebo," I say.

5 DECEMBER 2010

Invasion of the Land Prawns

Today, after a four-hour drive from Kampala (average speed, 120 kilometers per hour — seriously), I had lunch with a Ugandan friend I haven't seen in several months. She brought me a gift: a plastic bag full of fried, salted grasshoppers. Turns out they're more addictive than Fritos Corn Chips and certainly more nutritious. Crunch, crunch. I can't get enough of the little suckers. I think of them as Land Prawns. I'm popping them by the palm-full right now as I write this, washing them down with Nile Lager. Good lord, they are tasty.

There is some kind of perfect logic to eating them here in this Rwenzori Mountains town of Fort Portal at this very time because the place is currently inundated with the wee beasts. As mentioned in the previous essay about the Kampala mosque, there were a lot in the big, crazy city, but that was nothing compared to here.

It's like a remake of Hitchcock's "The Birds," but with grasshoppers, or that exquisitely constructed scene from Terrence Malick's "Days of Heaven." You know the one: First, a lone grasshopper appears on a head of cabbage in the kitchen, then there are 100 billion blanketing the wheat fields and Richard Gere is going all un-Buddhist hysterical trying to get rid of the little winged Lucifers.

Everywhere I go here they are literally in my face, in my bed, down my shirt and covering entire buildings. I took a bunch of macro photos of them, which gave me the opportunity to get a very close look. They are Martians. Also, when they get freaked out, they jump, often at your face. But once you realize they're just harmless hysterics (like Richard Gere in "Days of Heaven"), it doesn't bother you.

16 DECEMBER 2010

Trans-Uganda Sutra

We drive halfway across Uganda every four to six weeks, from the west to Kampala and back again. Farouk or Saturday or Moses at the wheel.

The villages are now familiar, the landscape well known.

We go for long stretches without talking, sometimes listening to music or the play-by-play of soccer games, sometimes not.

Our discussions range from Wayne Rooney's female troubles to whether Museveni will be reelected (does a zebra have stripes?), the difference in the price of matooke between Mubende and Kampala, what meat makes the best muchomo, and why I like Aziz Azion's slow songs.

I often lapse into a sort of dream, gazing out the windows at the verdant farmland that carpets rural Uganda, the dancing dogs, the satin, brocade and plaid.

Now there's a shrieking girl or a blue umbrella, a camel, a car spinning out of control. Then they're gone. Next comes the rain. And the dust. A cloud of grasshoppers. An elephant.

The abundance of images rapidly flickering by induces a stoned, cinematic state. Are you getting this? Yes, yes, I am. I think so.

We are in a corridor of ephemeral visions. Each wall is a filmstrip. The pictures that flash past pile up chaotically: An incongruent, subconscious attachment to the dreaminess. I've got it all.

On the last couple of trips, I've passed the time by making photographs as we moved, trying to capture the visions floating by, straight ahead, to the right, to the left. I'll show you when we get there ...

31 DECEMBER 2010

Simba's Kapchorwa by Night

"My father was called Simba," the large man standing in front of me says. "It was a nickname. And now that he's gone, you can call me Simba." He adjusts the position of his white cap and straightens his cuffs.

"OK, I will."

Simba owns Noah's Ark Hotel in Kapchorwa, Eastern Uganda, in the dramatically beautiful Mount Elgon/Sipi Falls region near the Kenya border. I spoke with him very briefly when we first arrived, as he handed out pieces of candy to all 35 of my traveling companions who joined me on this work trip. Simba likes to hand out candy wherever he goes. He is the quintessential hail-fellow-well-met evangelist for good cheer and high times as he moves about this small, high-mountain community where he grew up, and where his 65-year-old mother is still producing 100 bags of coffee a year. He is a dynamo of jocularity and commerce; born to be an innkeeper.

The next time I encounter Simba, late afternoon the day after we arrive, he tells me he needs my advice about the position of a new fireplace. "I want your opinion, your architectural expertise. I think they put it in the wrong place. Please, come with me over to my new hotel. We'll go, have a beer, come right back. I will buy your beer. You can have one or two, no charge. How many do you want?"

"I think one will do the trick," I say. I explain that I have no architectural expertise, but Simba's not having it.

"If you change your mind and want two, you can have two."

"OK, thanks."

The man is a funnel cloud of charm and charisma, benign manipulation and big fun. All around him are pulled into the cloud. He's his own 24-7 entertainment channel, in 3-D. He cajoles, flatters, feigns hurt, all to get what he wants at the price he wants it. He's very effective. He now owns three hotels and a nightclub. But today he's going to work his magic on two women selling bunches of matooke at the roadside.

I've been here long enough to know that no one has a beer and comes right back. Ever. Especially if you are in the company of a man called Simba. But he's just not a guy you can or want to say no to. So here I am waiting in his luxury van as he first praises then scolds the matooke ladies.

The negotiation is starting to drag on and I get out to watch. One woman wants 500 shillings (about 25 cents) more than Simba wants to pay. At one point he looks like he's about to start crying, then he turns on his heel and storms away, then he pivots again, huge Cheshire smile lighting up the entire hillside and all but begs her to drop the price. Finally he cocks his handsome head flirtatiously to one side and says, "Pleeeezzze," in English. The woman finds this hysterically funny and crumbles. Simba gets his matooke.

At the gate to the Noah's Ark Hotel No. 2 the driver lays on the horn and two security guards open up and let us drive in. Simba sends one of them to get me a cold Club beer. "Come," he says, "look at the fireplace."

The outside of the single-story house is painted with pictures of animals, but the inside is still being finished. He's exercised about the fireplace because it's in the middle of the wall and makes the corner areas on either side of it unusable. "What do you think?" he asks solemnly. Two bricklayers are standing next to us.

"Why don't you put it in the corner?" I say.

"Great idea! Of course," he says, looking at the bricklayers with a why-didn't-you-think-of-that squint. "Now what about the chimney?"

The hole for the chimney has already been cut in the ceiling. "Well, you've got the Noah's Ark thing going, how about curving the chimney over from the corner, plaster the brick and have your artist paint a snake on it?"

"Yes, yes, yes," he says. "Take this one out," he tells the bricklayers, pointing at the nearly complete fireplace, "and make it over in the corner instead."

"A quarter round shape might look good," I say, showing the contour by sweeping my hand between the two right-angle walls.

"Quarter round shape," Simba tells the bricklayers. "Make the chimney a snake." And we leave.

"OK, we'll just drop the matooke by my other hotel, then we'll go back," Simba says.

His third and oldest hotel is also the funkiest, geared toward backpackers and locals. We pull up in front, the matooke is carried in, Simba bickers and banters with the staff, hands out candy to several guests seated in the cafe and we depart.

"I want you to see my sports and entertainment center," he says. "It is just two blocks away. We go, we look, and you'll be back before dinner is served."

It's a big place on Kapchorwa's main street. Simba leads me in and starts passing out candy to the 20 or so men sitting on couches watching football. He pays special attention to five men seated against the back wall, shaking each one's hand, giving each extra candy. "These ones don't hear," he says. "These are deaf."

Simba walks through a doorway to the bar and continues to the large room at the back of the building. It's dark and filled with young men standing around brightly lit pool tables. There is loud music and the steady, noisy knocking of pool balls. "Oh," he says to me, "I think we have time for a game of pool, don't we?"

"Yeah, I think so," I say. "You play, I'll take pictures."

Simba hands out more candy, grabs a pool cue out of someone's hand and steps to a table where a game is already underway. "Won't you have another Club?" he asks me. "My treat, have two."

"I'm good as is," I say.

The balls are collected and racked up and Simba makes the break. A young friend of his steps forward and sinks three balls. The kid is talented. Simba twirls on his heel and mugs as if he's terrified, then puts a ball in the side pocket. The kid raises his eyebrows.

"You know, I stopped drinking two years ago," Simba tells me, "because I was always buying people drinks, but they never bought me drinks. So I stopped. Now I just drink coffee."

"Can I buy you a coffee?" I say.

"No, I won't sleep if I drink it this late. Besides, this is my place. I don't have to buy it here. It's already my coffee."

Simba is a loud, theatrical pool player. For him, pool is as physical a sport as soccer. What he lacks in skill, he more than makes up for with a symphony of hoots, whistles, hisses, howls, lunges with the cue stick, dance steps and various other calisthenics that entertain everyone nearby, but don't win him the game. He buys the kid a beer

for beating him and asks me, "Don't you think I'm the world's best pool player?"

"You're definitely the noisiest," I say. He laughs so hard at this remark he seems to stop breathing for a moment.

He recovers and we leave, Simba passing out candy as we go, stopping to give three more pieces each to the deaf men.

"How long have you owned the hotel where I'm staying?" I ask him.

"Ten years," he says. "I started it with $2."

"Really?" I say.

"Sure," Simba says.

11 JANUARY 2011

The Big Dog Comes to the Village

President Museveni made a campaign appearance in our little burg last Saturday. We pulled out the stops — drumming, dancing, singing, speeches, more speeches, dozens of plainclothes security guys cruising the crowd, the obligatory brain-blasting sound system and jillions of yellow T-shirts (yellow is the color of Museveni's party, the National Resistance Movement, formerly the National Resistance Army — back in the days of the bush war that brought him to power).

Museveni was several hours late, but that did little to dampen the spirit of the crowd. Ugandans are expert at patiently waiting for hours and hours. It's a good thing, because that's how long most things take here.

Before he arrived there was a parade and performances by music and dancing groups. That was the high point for me. That and getting pestered by the security guys.

They must breed them on one big ranch somewhere that supplies all the security guys for all the big shots on earth, because whether you're here or in San Jose you can pick them out of a crowd from a mile away. But the Ugandan ones are different than, say, the U.S. Secret Service. The Ugandans are an easy laugh. I've tried to joke with U.S. Secret Service guys. Not.

Seems the officers at Saturday's event were convinced I had a camera. I didn't. I'd taken it home before coming into the stage area. But they needed to ask me 14 times before I think they maybe, possibly started to believe that, in fact, I did not have a camera. There were three of them and just as they were dialing back the third-degree treatment, I decided to turn things around, lighten the vibe.

"Do you have a camera?" I asked security guy No.1.

"How about you?" I said to No. 2. "I think you might have a camera."

Then I asked No. 3. "And if you do," I said, "loan it to me so I can take some pictures. C'mon, I'll give it back. I'm the only muzungu here. It's not like you're gonna have a hard time finding me in the crowd."

At that point they all started laughing and I started laughing and the sun broke through the clouds and I think I could hear an angel choir singing. I was going to ask them if they heard it, but I decided not to push my luck. No. 2 told me to have a nice afternoon and the three of them went off to hassle someone even more suspicious-looking than me, though I doubt there was any such person in the crowd.

As for the president, I split before he showed and before I got sunstroke, but the sound system was so frickin' loud I could clearly hear his speech while stretched out on my bed in the cool comfort of my house … with my camera.

4 FEBRUARY 2011

Zanzibar Moon Breathing

The full moon sprays across Matemwe Beach on the east coast of Zanzibar.

The shells and coral fragments and the sugary sand all catch the light and bounce it everywhere. The water resembles sloshing mercury. Then there's the air.

The air is warm, but not too warm; cool but not too cool. It's sexy, sleepy, soothing. It is infused with centuries' worth of cloves and cardamom and cinnamon and pepper, vanilla and coconut. And devils and angels, good times, bad times.

The air is filled with longing and wistfulness. One breathes in a profound emotional force here. There is a massive, nearly unbearable weight in the poignant legacy of this place. You inhale it on a night like tonight. On any night. Zanzibar was, for hundreds of years, a center for the buying and selling of humans. Multiple millions of hearts (not to mention minds and bodies) were broken here.

But the air and the water and the great glowing sphere make all that disappear tonight. Only the sensuality and kindness of the landscape exist right now. The moonlight washes away everything else — including memory.

7 FEBRUARY 2011

Journey to No Name Island

Actually, you can call it Magnificent Lunch Island. I can't remember its real name, if it had one, and that one better suits it because that is what happened there.

Two of us and four crew members, most of whom turned out to be cooks, climbed in a small open boat on a sweltering, blustery day and set out for an uninhabited dot of forest-covered land about an hour from Zanzibar. The water was relatively calm when we launched, but it started to kick up a fuss at about the halfway point — nothing major, just enough to give the ride some dramatic tension.

Once we got there, you could see Zanzibar across the sloshing channel. It wasn't a big island. You couldn't have fit a Wal-Mart parking lot on it, but it did have a single, portly baobab tree, which was also the location of the kitchen.

After we waded through waist-deep water to shore, the cooks got to work. Some friends of theirs showed up in a second boat and one went spear fishing, bringing up two octopus and five polychrome fish that were too good-looking to eat, though we did anyway. One of the men cleaned the fish down on the rocks by the water. Another man started a fire, filled a pot half-full of coconut oil, and put the pot on the fire.

He'd brought a bucket full of potatoes sliced into French fries and he proceeded to make the most heartbreakingly good chips (as they are called here) that I've ever eaten. And there were a lot of them.

Lobster and calamari and plenty of limes and some kind of supernaturally good mango chutney concoction had also come with us.

The lobster and calamari were grilled over one fire while the fish and octopus were done on another. It was all staggeringly delicious, but the octopus was so good I almost passed out.

After lunch, as the tide continued to recede, a sandbar that extended from the north end of the island began to emerge from the waves, like a submarine surfacing.

It was smooth when it first appeared, but after a few minutes, dozens of small holes and mounds of sand appeared. Crabs the size of soup bowls were scampering hither and thither, digging holes as if they were dogs and watching us carefully with their eyes, which they kept at the end of long stalks.

27 FEBRUARY 2011

Scenes From a Zanzibar January

The Africa Hotel on the Stone Town waterfront has been a favorite drinking establishment of expats and tourists and well-heeled locals since the bad old days of colonialism. The Brits knew how to site a bar. The place has a large balcony jutting out from the front of the building, affording an exquisite sunset view of the dhow harbor where many of the fishermen tie up their sailing vessels. Across the street and next to the sea wall is a small, triangular grassy area where people hang out, play music and apparently sell illicit substances. I met a Rastafarian-looking fellow named Simon there and we had a brief conversation. It went like so:

Simon: "Greetings. I have Malawi for sale."

Me: "Wow! The entire country?"

Simon: "No, Malawi. Grass. Marijuana." (Later I did an extensive survey and could find no one who had heard of calling pot "Malawi.")

Me: "I don't smoke the stuff, Simon. I don't like the high."

Simon: "Yeah, you're too old."

Me: "Could be. How old are you? You don't exactly look like a pup yourself."

Simon: "42."

Me: "I was smoking pot before you were born!"

Simon: "See, I'm right. Hey, I've got a boat. I could take you out in it."

Me: "OK, if I need to go out in a boat, maybe I'll come find you. You don't think I'm too old for that, huh?"

Simon: "No, you're not too old to go in a boat."

Me: "But too old to smoke Malawi?"

Simon: "In a boat? You should not smoke it in a boat. You might fall over. My stuff, you will definitely fall over."

While walking through Jozani forest, under the tall, tall, tall mahogany trees, I see an aquamarine tree snake about two feet long stretched languorously on the branch of a dead bush. It holds its head up, suddenly alert, tracking me as I walk by like one of those motion-sensor burglar alarms. Meanwhile, at my feet, in a hole beneath a log, is a freshwater crab. A blade of grass is stuck in the hole and the crab rushes out to grab it, and then retreats just as quickly.

Farther down the path red colobus monkeys are chillaxin' in small trees, reclining on branches three or four feet off the ground.

They are habituated to humans and don't move even when I step within a couple of feet to take a photo — babies keep nursing, couples keep grooming, one old dozing gentleman can barely open his eyes.

Nearby is the Zanzibar Butterfly Center, a large, netted walk-through zoo and breeding facility for indigenous butterflies that has proven to be a significant moneymaker for the local farmers who participate in its programs. As we're shown around, we run into a large praying mantis and a friend tells this story:

"When I was a young girl, my mother always told me that if the praying mantis looked directly at me I would not grow breasts.

"'You will be a woman,' my mother said, 'but you will look like a man!'

"So I always took care to walk behind the praying mantises."

"But now that you have breasts you can walk in front of them?"

"Sure."

I'm watching yet another sunset from my hotel's treehouse bar at the drunkenly named village of Bububu, and what should come on the CD player but Bobby Womack's long, beautifully gritty ballad "Across 110th Street." It is so incongruent, so inappropriate to the moment that it is just right and perfect in every way as it ushers the sun off the edge of the earth with grace, soul and Womack's ghetto howl from across the world.

SYED BARGHASH BIN SAID, SULTAN OF ZANZIBAR.

7 DECEMBER 2011

The Sultan's Portrait

The labyrinthine streets of Zanzibar's Stone Town — the whole of which is a UNESCO World Heritage Site — are just wide enough to accommodate a pedestrian and a motorcycle, provided the pedestrian leaps into a doorway when the motorcycle rockets past.

Zanzibar is approximately 98 percent Muslim, and one of the first things you notice as you drive into Stone Town, which is the only city on the 50-mile-long island, is many, many women wearing the full veil. For a Westerner, it is one among several characteristics that give this profoundly historical place a surreal, time-out-of-time atmosphere. The seemingly endless maze of streets you wander once you're in the city center is another.

The narrowness of the streets, combined with the ancient multi-story buildings lining both sides, makes sense because the sweltering sun can penetrate for only minutes a day, leaving the citizens to walk the merchant alleys in blessed shade most of the time. The shops that line these thoroughfares sell kanga cloth and sandals, carvings and curios, oddities and spices, even some old engravings. There are also hair salons, many of which offer henna ornamentation for the hands, the feet, the back and anywhere else a client wishes to be decorated with one of the world's oldest forms of temporary tattoo.

I walked in one shop because I'm a fan of old prints and there were several hanging on the entry door. They appeared to be engravings from old newspapers, fine, dark lines of crosshatching and precise details on yellowed paper — images of tribal warriors brandishing spears at men in pith helmets, elephants being attacked by lions, and various long-forgotten Middle Eastern potentates, wearing turbans and jewels and with great curving knives stuck in their brocade cummerbunds.

There was a room at the back of the store, but it was unlit and I could barely see inside. When I stood at the entry to the room, however, I could see there were what looked like several pages torn from magazines or newspapers, very old, piled on a table.

My cellphone has a little flashlight on it, so I flicked that on and went into the room to take a look. What I'd seen were indeed magazine pages, and one was nearly 136 years old — from the "Supplement to the London Illustrated News, June 19, 1875." It featured an oval portrait of Syed Barghash bin Said, the second Sultan of Zanzibar, and below that a picture of the "Arctic Search-Ship Pandora." Wikipedia has a lengthy, thorough entry about Barghash, mentioning that he "ruled Zanzibar from October 7, 1870 to March 26, 1888," and "is credited with building much of the infrastructure of Stone Town, including piped water, public baths, a police force, roads, parks, hospitals and large administrative buildings such as the (Bait el-Ajaib) House of Wonders." (The House of Wonders still stands. It is now the National Museum and is full of wonders.)

More important for incurable romantics, Barghash was the brother of Sayyida Salme (later Emily Ruete), the star-crossed princess who married a German soldier and either ran off or was run off to Germany, where he died young leaving her with several children and no country; she was a pariah in Zanzibar. Though she did return for two visits after her husband's death, she was never accepted and died in Germany at age 79.

"I've gotta have this picture of the Sultan," I told the young shopkeeper.

"No," he said. "That's not for sale. We need that."

"I need it more, for an old friend, a long ways away."

"Really? You do?"

"Yes, I do. Definitely."

He hemmed and hawed and finally relented, charged me a couple bucks and sent me off with the Sultan and the Arctic Search-Ship Pandora tucked in my bag.

THE ARCTIC SEARCH-SHIP PANDORA.

9 MARCH 2011

In the Caves of the Shetani Cult

I had a phone number for the overseer of Ufufuma Forest in the center of Zanzibar. I called several times, but never got an answer. Finally, I decided to go there, take my chances. The forest is about an hour by car from where I was staying. Nasser, the driver, knew the area and was willing to take me, so off we went.

I'd read about the shetani years ago and then again on the plane to Zanzibar. I was intrigued when I heard that it's possible to visit the shetani cult's ceremonial caves on the island.

In "Zanzibar: The Bradt Travel Guide," Gemma Pitcher writes, "According to local traditional beliefs, shetani are creatures from another world, living on earth alongside animals and humans, but invisible most of the time and generally ill-intentioned. Many of the ebony carvings on sale in Zanzibar's curio shops depict the various forms a shetani can take — for example, a hunched and hideously twisted old woman, a man-dog hybrid, or a young girl with the legs of a donkey.

"There is no real way, say the locals, of protecting yourself from the possibility of being haunted or attacked by a shetani. ... Should the worst happen ... and a shetani decides to take up residence in your home – or even, in the worst case scenario, your body – the only thing to be done is to visit a mganga (sorcerer)."

In Zanzibar, many of the mganga live around Ufufuma Forest. Their places of business are the subterranean caves in the thick woods. After failing to reach the fellow in charge of visiting the caves, I asked around and was told I should just go to the village of Jendele and see if I could get someone there to guide me into the forest.

A small, rusty sign dangling by the roadside is the only indication that you're approaching Ufufuma Forest and moments later a few buildings appear on either side of the road — Jendele. We stopped. There were a couple of young guys leaning against a tree and I suggested to Nasser that he go over and ask if they'd take us to the caves. I know even less Swahili than Lhukonzo, so I was not up to trying to negotiate a price with them. Nasser wasn't either, it turned out. After five minutes of heated discussion, he came back to the car and told me they wanted 150,000 TZ shillings to guide us. "That's absurd," I said. "That's a non-starter." Nasser and I had a brief, complicated discussion about what non-starter meant and then I got out of the car and motioned for the two aspiring robbers to come over and talk. As they ambled to the car, I asked Nasser to translate.

"All I've got is 20,000," I said, pulling the bill from my shirt pocket. "If you can't do it for that, we'll have to leave without seeing the caves. That would be a shame, don't you think?"

John, the bigger of the two guys, spoke intensely to Nasser for several minutes. "What's he say?" I asked.

"He says, 'Let's go.'"

I handed John the 20,000 note and he and his friend led us past a few houses and into a warren of narrow trails lined with chest-high brush. It was hot and humid and I kept running into spider webs face-first. It cooled very slightly as we approached the forest and the tall trees became more abundant, and then even more so, until it got downright crowded. The foliage blocked much of the light.

Just as I was wondering where the two were really taking us, John looked back at me and pointed ahead at a large black hole in a big rock. There seemed to be red and white flags hung around it and inside of it.

At the entrance, I could see the hole went almost straight down. There appeared to be a stream at the bottom. More red and white flags hung from the short stalactites on the cave's ceiling. John went in. Nasser stepped down and motioned for me to follow him.

It was a steep, mossy non-staircase. We got about halfway down and John took a small waragi bottle off a ledge and held it out to me. "What is it?" I asked Nasser.

He conferred with John. "He says it's ground-up human bone."

"Oh," I said.

Once we got down inside the cavern, John pointed out the flowing stream and said it connected several of the caves. "Let's see some others," I said.

In the Bradt guide, Pitcher explains, "Each mganga is in contact with ten or so shetani, who can be instructed to drive out other shetani from someone who is possessed, or to work their power in favour of the customer. The waganga are also herbalists, preparing healing medicines where spirit possession is not indicated, or combining both physical and occult treatment in severe cases.

"But there are some shetani, goes the current thinking, which even a mganga cannot control. The latest and most famous of these was (or is) Popo Bawa — a phenomenon of far greater significance than just a run-of-the-mill shetani, which gripped Zanzibar's population in a wave of mass hysteria in 1995."

The panic generated by Popo Bawa — Swahili for "bat wing" — escalated over weeks into a crowd madness that culminated in the beating death of a handicapped man, who people believed was possessed by the shetani. After that, Pitcher writes, "the hysteria abated somewhat and Popo Bawa retreated. He is widely expected to return, however."

John led us to three or four other caves, some smaller, some larger. All had the red and white flags that symbolized something, but I'll be damned if I can remember what.

Apparently, if you make advance arrangements, and if you're prepared to be flexible about time and, you know, everything, you can, for a fee, observe the ceremonies.

As we walked back to the village, I talked with John; Nasser translated. "So the mganga live near here?" I asked. "But who are they?"

"They're our fathers," John said.

13 MARCH 2011

The Way of the Dhow

Before you ever get a close look, you see them far away, out across the sloshing cerulean prairie, beneath the brutish and insistent sun. They don't sail so much as skate. They skate and slide and slip sideways like a water strider in a cross current. And when the wind stops they do not, they don't even slow; they continue gliding across the Indian Ocean as if they are not subject to the laws of physics. They bounce and bob in the sun and rain like a happy animal in familiar surroundings. They shiver a little as the gusts pick up again. Then the winds come on in earnest, the sails puff out like a rooster's chest, and black, black men, as graceful and measured in their movements as Astaire, waltz across the dipping, twisting decks, lean into the wind, pull and push to make it home before the flood of darkness drowns them in dreams.

The dhows of Zanzibar, handmade sailing boats — some large, some smallish — that are used for transport and shipping and fishing, are one of the great kinetic (and pragmatic) sculptures of the modern African world. Like many other things here they have changed little in a century or two or nine. Actually, I just looked that up; make it the first century AD, and long before that, no doubt.

There are nearly as many websites as there are fish in the sea, taking up every subject you can think of and many you can't. Or shouldn't. Naturally, there is one about ancient navigation and sailing, and of course it has a page on "The History and Construction of the Dhow," which is where I found this:

"The dhow was known for two distinctive features. First of all, its triangular or lateen sail, and secondly, for its stitched construction. Stitched boats were made by sewing the hull boards together with fibers, cords or thongs.

"The idea of a boat made up of planks sewn together seems strange. Actually, it is a type that has been in wide use in many parts of the world and in some places still is. In the Indian Ocean, it dominated the waters right up to the fifteenth century, when the arrival of the Portuguese opened the area to European methods. A Greek sea captain or merchant who wrote in the first century AD reports the use of small sewn boats off Zanzibar and off the southern coast of Arabia. Marco Polo saw sewn boats at Hormuz at the entrance to the Persian Gulf. He took a dim view of them: "they were [held together by] twine and with it they stitch the planks of the ship together. It keeps well and is not corroded by sea-water but it will not stand well in a storm."

(Marco Polo, incidentally, kicked it from 1254 or thereabouts to January 8, 1324. He died 611 years to the day before Elvis was born!)

Anyway, where was I? Dhows, yes. I got a little obsessed with the boats on Zanzibar. It was a treat to walk the bleached-flour beaches, where the tide goes out and out and out, so a vast squishy plain is revealed and you can stroll among the temporarily stuck wooden vessels (being oh so careful not to step on the sea urchins) and closely examine the construction of them. They are exquisite. Any wood sculptor would be envious of the great craft, care and precision with which they are fit together. And the way they move on the water must impress even the dolphins, judging by the dances of appreciation they perform as the dhows pass by.

18 MARCH 2011

Shoes and Elephants

The last leg of the journey from town to the village where I live is a dirt road that winds through a few other villages, past cotton fields at the low elevation, and coffee orchards as it climbs up into the mountains.

It takes 30 to 40 minutes once you leave the pavement to follow the road all the way to my home. That is, unless you run into what we did a couple of days ago: a major jam-up of slow-moving, spectacularly horned cows with a few sheep bringing up the rear. There were several silent, bony dogs too. They were doing absolutely nothing to move things along.

The dramatic-looking Ankole cattle graze here and there in various uncultivated fields and along the roadside. They are carefully watched over, as getting into the farmers' fields would not go down well. Not at all. That's left to the elephants. They like to dine in the dark.

The other day, Biira, a shopkeeper I know, came into my office visibly upset. I asked her what was wrong. "Last night the elephants ate my parents' cassava field and most of the pineapple."

"I'm surprised they ate the pineapple," I said.

"Yes, and I had a field of my own there too, of beans."

Biira's parents live in the lowlands a few miles downhill from the village. They are subsistence farmers and they grow cotton as a cash crop. Losing an acre or more of cassava is an enormous blow. It means they will have to use some of the little money they bring in from the cotton to buy food.

The elephants wander out of the national park after the sun goes down, enticed by the crops that are just across the road. In theory, the government will reimburse farmers for losses, but from what I hear, actually penetrating the unfathomable bureaucracy and getting paid is a wee bit complicated. As in, forget it.

"What will your parents do?" I asked.

"Well," Biira said, "they went to town today to sell their shoes."

21 APRIL 2011

Love and Money

I was happy to hear that my young friend Doviko would be marrying his true love, Rosemary, but a little surprised when he recently asked for my help in purchasing her. I will be sending him a 50,000 shilling contribution later today.

The tradition of the bride price in Uganda is a teeny bit controversial, though it shows no signs of going away any time soon. Indeed, just last year, Uganda's Constitutional Court rejected a petition to abolish it with a 4-to-1 vote (three of those votes were cast by women judges; the lone dissenting judge was a man).

At the time, Hillary Nsambu wrote a reasonably thorough discussion of the matter in the New Vision newspaper, a government-supported publication. "The petitioners of a Tororo-based lobby group, who were represented by 13 people, including a Roman Catholic priest," Nsambu explained, "had asked the court to abolish bride price, commonly known as dowry, arguing that it was degrading and caused domestic violence."

One of the judges who voted down the petition, Laetitia Kikonyogo, said, "The court cannot say with certainty that bride price [is] unconstitutional on such a ground, because there are varied and numerous causes of spousal abuse." It is, Kikonyogo argued, a couple's "constitutional right to choose the way they would wish to get married."

Further in the article, Nsumba writes, "Justice Mpagi-Bahigeine said the court should not be quick to slap a blanket ban on bride price as it would rob the various ethnic groups of their identity, dignity and self-worth. 'These customs are value systems, which only a particular tribe best knows. I think, therefore, that they ought to be allowed to keep what they treasure,' Mpagi-Bahigeine said ... Justice Kavuma, on his part, described the term bride price as bride wealth. In his view, there was nothing unconstitutional about bride wealth as a requirement for marriage."

It gets complicated. Like so many African cultural traditions, it cannot be viewed through the lens of, say, American social customs with any degree of clarity. Western-style feminism does not directly translate to this context. Women in the remote, rural area where I live, for example, are hardly meek, wimpy little flowers. They are tough, sweet, earthy, outspoken and profound realists in a way that only a subsistence farmer can be. The things that concern them the most are issues like shared land title and getting adequate (or any) medical care for their children and themselves. From what I can tell, doing away with bride price is far down on their list of priorities.

In any case, the ways in which love and money are entangled throughout the world are rarely clear. What is commerce and what's not is usually more conversation than question. By the way, the budget Doviko gave me refers to "bride wealth" and "thanks giving to bride's parents." The term "bride price" isn't used. Perhaps change is coming to the back country.

18 MAY 2011

Pigmalion

Ah, pigs! They exude an undeniable charm, a certain je ne sais quoi that is irresistible. They are so piggish and not at all self-conscious about it; so authentic, so comfortable in their own pigskin. It's a special kind of elegance, a kind that allows you to sleep blissfully in a mound of trash while first flapping your left ear and then your right — in a futile but entertaining attempt to chase away flies.

Pigs are a regular and frequent feature of my life now. They are everywhere in the village. They are the sanitation department, carefully sorting through the garbage piles, organizing, snorting appreciatively, gobbling up the goodies.

Some walk around freely on garbage patrol, others are tied by a cord around one ankle. There are a few very big pigs and many piglets. A favorite among the larger porkers is the one tied behind Medius' store most afternoons. I call him Road Block Pig. No matter which side of my commute path he's tied on, he must strain at his tether to eat something almost out of reach on the other side. When I want to pass, I clap at him and he glares up at me, looks annoyed, and slowly shifts into reverse.

But the most memorable hoglet of all has become something of a visual icon, or at least its face has, a reference often cited by me and a dear friend of mine here to illustrate our piggish tendencies. I saw it on a morning like any other when I was walking to work. I was following my commute path that passes through people's yards and behind shops, past fields and latrines and garbage pits. As I walked past one rubbish-filled hole, I looked down to see a very small piglet. It had its head happily and enthusiastically buried in half of an avocado — they grow them big here, nearly the size of footballs.

For some reason this particular avocado had been tossed when its interior was still largely intact and this particular piglet was the lucky beneficiary. When the piglet heard me, it glanced up and a visual icon was born. Its entire face was coated with light green avocado, as if it was in the middle of a spa treatment, a facial. And through the green I could see its little blinking piglet eyes. And in those dewy eyes I saw true, indelible, indisputable, undiluted joy. And whenever I think of that avocado green face looking up at me, I feel the same way.

27 JUNE 2011

The Sensuous Rhino

To be splashed with warm equatorial mud by a rhinoceros luxuriating in a shallow puddle is, it turns out, one of life's rare pleasures. Very rare.

Even though I was wearing a new shirt, a clean shirt, purchased just the day before at the Garden City shopping mall in Kampala, I didn't mind too much. I savored it, actually.

How often in life does one get to stand within 5 feet of a rhinoceros while it bathes in Ugandan mud? Not often at all.

And in this case it was two rhinos.

There was, however, a problem, a very rhino-centric limitation that prevented the two from experiencing the unmitigated pleasure they were seeking. The horns. Both rhinos wanted to roll over onto their backs. But both rhinos could not do so. They tried, but they could not. It was an understandable desire: They wanted to get the acreage that constituted their backs wet with warm mud. But if you are a very large rhino in a not so big puddle, and you are bathing in the company of another large rhino, and you have a large horn with a slight curve in it growing from the top of your more than ample snout, rolling onto your back is not one of the options available to you.

So you resign yourself to getting your vast expanse of belly nicely mud-soaked, and to getting your stubby but powerful legs well muddied, and to rolling your whisker-covered chinny-chin-chin on the muddy bank.

And you call it a day. With much straining and slipping and grunting, you get up and out. But before you do, you shake your great torso. And any creature standing nearby, within 5 feet or so, gets thoroughly sprayed with mud, even if he is wearing a new shirt, a clean shirt, purchased just the day before at the Garden City shopping mall in Kampala.

5 AUGUST 2011

The Apartheid Museum, Johannesburg

A lot has changed in South Africa since apartheid ended in 1994, and a lot hasn't. The whites got to keep their mansions and Mercedes and the blacks got to keep their servant uniforms and the right to operate leaf blowers on the vast lawns surrounding the giant houses in the tony neighborhoods like the one where I stayed: Pretoria's Brooklyn suburb.

To be fair, staying where I did gave me a slightly skewed view of the country, but not that skewed. There is still a vast gap separating black and white — socially and economically — and it is apparent wherever you look.

Pretoria and Johannesburg are about 30 or 40 minutes apart. Jo'burg is the financial center of Africa, while Pretoria is the quieter, low-key university town. Both cities are luxurious at the center (Pretoria resembles San Diego sans beach) and in their close-in, predominantly white suburbs, but farther out, in the townships and shanty settlements, life seems to have improved little over the last 17 years.

The ravages of apartheid and its precursor, colonialism, are everywhere evident, but not everything can be blamed on those twin scourges. Like much of the rest of Africa, it's now the colonialism within — the ferocious corruption and exploitation presided over by the black ruling class — that is in danger of destroying the hope that Mandela and many others gave to the country. The education system is, apparently, dead on its feet. So, developing a broad middle class that does not comprise merely a few elites is still only a vague aspiration.

On balance, there is a black middle class and it has grown since 1994, but poverty is still severe and widespread — shameful for a country with the wealth, resources and infrastructure of South Africa. According to the official statistic, about a quarter of the population is unemployed, but judging from the number of obviously idle young people, and not so young people, that figure can't have much in common with reality. President Jacob Zuma and his cohorts in the African National Congress have a lot to answer for. What will happen once the enormously influential presence of Mandela is no more is an unsettling question.

One day while I was there, after a lunch of prosciutto and kalamata olive pizza at a shopping mall that would not have looked out of place in Beverly Hills or Boca Raton, I took a taxi to the Apartheid Museum.

I first went through the special exhibit on Mandela's life; he'd turned 93 the week before and Michelle Obama had stopped by to visit him. I then took another two and a half hours to view the museum's permanent exhibits, an exhaustive, text-heavy, extremely well put together and, needless to say, intense linear narrative of the rise and fall of apartheid.

Afterward, I sat in the hip little cafe and had an expensive latte with a biscotti, then walked over to the museum gift shop. It seemed like some kind of Mel Brooksian parody — apartheid-themed souvenirs! There were coffee mugs, shoulder bags, hats and scarves, pens and posters. The clerk didn't glance up as I entered, walked around and exited. She was deeply immersed in "The Girl With the Dragon Tattoo."

24 SEPTEMBER 2011

The Gaze

Everywhere I go in this village, and much of the rest of Uganda, eyes follow me. I'm stared at intensely; everything I do is watched, scrutinized, commented on, laughed at or, if I, say, stumble or drop something, met with a chorus of "Sorry, sorry, sorry …"

It can get tedious. If you are bothered by the unrelenting gaze of others, Africa is maybe not the place for you — especially if you are a foreigner and noticeably different in appearance from most Africans. I, for example, am the only white person living in this village; there's not another muzungu for many kilometers, and sometimes weeks can go by before a foreigner visits.

I'm stared at because I'm a novelty, but I believe there's also another reason that has to do with the deep history of this place and the people who live here. It is a matter of language and memory.

Like most African languages, Lhukonzo has no means of notation, no written component, nor its own alphabet. Lhukonzo words were given alphabetic representation only after the arrival of foreigners, largely English-speaking. Many of the people, perhaps most, in the region where I live can neither read nor write. Information is conveyed by word of mouth, gesture and often through the use of pictures.

So, when you can't rely on list making, on books, on the notation of memory-jogging phrases, how do you reinforce recollection? One good method is to develop an extraordinary visual memory. People who have not had the benefit of a written language to supplement their memory might, over the generations, become extremely adept at recording mental pictures. And, in addition to mere curiosity, it is that facility, I believe, that is partly responsible for the African gaze, the endless stare, collecting every visual detail.

I'm frequently amazed by the minute visual differences friends here notice. A few weeks ago, I replaced my cellphone with a new one exactly like it. The one I replaced was still fairly new itself, but it had developed an unfixable technical problem, likely due to the fact that it's one of the cheapest phones available here. The old phone and the new phone were identical. The first day I had the new phone, I pulled it out to use it and a village woman standing nearby, someone I see maybe once a week, said, "Ah, you have a new phone."

That night, I put the new phone and the old phone on the table and looked at them closely. I could see no difference. None. Indeed, I turned on what I thought was the new one — just to be sure I wasn't putting the wrong phone back in my pocket. It's a good thing I checked: I'd picked up the old phone by mistake. And there have been many other similar occurrences here in which people have exhibited an uncanny ability to recall the smallest details of appearance.

So now, even when the unbroken stare grows tiresome, I remind myself that it's not what we in the West interpret as bad manners. It's intensely focused visual listening.

31 DECEMBER 2011

Johnnie Sits Down

"Once you've had a real taste of Africa," Johnnie says, "you'll find it quite hard to go back to, you know, the square world."

Johnnie calls the First World the square world. He talks like an old hipster, which he is — an old British hipster. Johnnie's got some money, maybe a lot of money. And he's still got his looks, a silver hedge of shaggy hair that falls over his collar, considerable charm, wry humor and a half-full bottle of Grant's 25-year-old scotch whisky that he carries with him from table to table as he chats up the clientele. He's somewhere between 70 and 80, I'm guessing, but still showing the vestiges of dapperness in an expat-going-to-seed sort of way. He's wearing black velveteen loafers, white socks, khaki safari shorts, a white shirt with a black vest and a dark blue ascot. Everything is rumpled and looks like it could use a laundering. But he makes it all work and he works it.

Johnnie sees me, walks directly to my table, sits down.

This bar and hotel are his wife's; she's Ugandan. Her name is Roberta. I stay here often enough coming through town on my way to and from Kampala, that Roberta now kisses me on both cheeks when I arrive. Johnnie is only around sometimes.

"I live in Nairobi, you see," he tells me early one evening as I pour myself shots from a pint bottle of J.W. Black and he serves himself from the triangular-shaped Grant's. "I just come here every three to four weeks to check in with Roberta."

"I suppose you have another wife in Nairobi," I joke.

"You're good," he says. "In fact, I do, and a third up in Senegal."

"That's gotta be tiring."

"You don't know the half of it, mate."

Johnnie staked Roberta to this place and she's made a thriving business of it, managing all the big stuff, but also arranging flower pots, checking the cleanliness of the glasses, ordering the staff about, and rushing down to the market to hand-pick tilapia for the kitchen. "You must have one of the fillets today," she says to me one morning. "Promise you will — with chips and kacumbari. And a Nile; Nile's on me."

"I promise, thanks." And I do and it is so tender and sweet and fresh that I almost burst into tears.

Over the course of several conversations and several days, I'm never quite able to extract from Johnnie what it was he did for a living before he retired, assuming he is retired.

"Business," he responds vaguely, "sometimes international business."

"What sort of business?"

"All sorts, you know, different things, rather boring, really. Care to shoot a little pool? Oh, your scotch has run out, poor fellow. Here, have some of mine." He pours about four shots of Grant's into my glass and walks to the pool table.

You could not cast Johnnie in a movie, could not use such a character in a novel. Just too cliché. Too much the rakish expatriate. You could if the novel were written by Somerset Maugham or Graham Greene or Ian Fleming 60 or so years ago, but not today.

"What do you do in Nairobi?"

"Not so much, really. See old friends, argue with the wife. I try to keep the arguments in English. When we argue in Swahili she reams me good and proper. One can't win when she's on with the Swahili. Don't even try. Just admit defeat and go to the bar until she's cooled down. Then come home, have sex. Cheaper than therapy and works better."

"There you go," I say.

"You break," Johnnie says.

I almost miss the cue ball, resulting in a pathetic break.

"I'm scared now," Johnnie says. "You need to start working out, mate."

"My hand slipped," I say. Johnnie raises his left eyebrow.

I'm not much of a pool player, it's true. But I soon realize that the problem of the moment is that I'm drunker than I thought I was when I was sitting down; standing up changes things, and not in a good way. A few more bad shots and I hand my cue to one of the young guys watching us play. It would be poor form to, say, rip the felt. "This gentleman is going to take over for me, Johnnie. I will go tend to the scotch."

"Don't drink it all, mate."

Fifteen minutes pass, he beats the kid, hands him a 2,000-shilling note to fund a couple more games, and comes back to the table.

"I know," he says. "Mine is an old, corny story. I came out not expecting to stay; I stayed. I hadn't planned to become a polygamist; just happened. This is another planet. I'm an alien here, but I like it too much to leave. Also, I can't afford to live in the square world. I have to stay."

"Do you still have family in the U.K.?"

"I do. We write occasionally, email these days, but haven't seen them in years. They never come here. They're scared."

"You've been here how long?"

"Thirty-two years, no, 34. I was 42 when I came."

"What's your favorite thing about Africa?"

"Besides the women?"

"Yes."

"The view. Looking out across vastness with no buildings, no roads."

"Yeah, I like that too. It always seems like something extraordinary is about to happen."

"Right," Johnnie says. "But it never does, does it? Freshen your drink, mate?"

15 JANUARY 2012

Ring of Fire

I stumbled upon a curious sight yesterday while walking home from work: people burning in hell at the behest of an evil monarch.

A Christian preacher accompanied by a music and theater group showed up in town last week and they've been giving live performances for the last few afternoons. They're so good I was almost born again. Almost.

I don't know who the props master is but he or she has done a brilliant job. The people who, thanks to a circle of woven dried banana tree leaves, were enveloped in a ring of fire (which definitely would not have received OSHA approval) were forced into that inferno by evil soldiers toting machine guns. The machine guns were crafted in great detail from banana tree stalks. (Unfortunately, everyone here is quite familiar with what machine guns look like.)

What was being acted out in this performance was the First Commandment: Thou shalt have no other gods before me (or words to that effect.) The bad soldiers were the henchmen of a king whom the good people wearing white refused to worship. The soldiers then cast them into the ring of fire. Much of the village stood around watching with fascination. Lighting the circle of banana leaves got some applause.

At one point — before she was thrown into the circle of flames — one of the girls dressed in white walked up to me, Bible open, and pointed toward the sky. I looked up. She looked up, moved on. I went to a nearby shop and bought four eggs, went home and boiled them — two for dinner, two for breakfast.

15 JANUARY 2012

The Hair in My Life

For someone with very little hair on his head, hair is a big part of my life.

It's a typical night: I'm sitting out in the courtyard — the usual balmy breeze blowing; bats fluttering about madly — reading William Boyd's superb "Brazzaville Beach," which I read 20-plus years ago, but remember nothing of. One of the benefits of a dissolving memory is that you get to read great books and enjoy them as if it were the first time!

Meanwhile, over at the table Enos built, Esther is doing young Lillian's hair while Asaba is assisting. This hairdo has taken at least 12 hours over two days and now Esther, and a preternaturally patient Lillian (Asaba's niece), are in the final minutes before completion.

Though in the photo it looks like they are about to ignite Lillian's head, what's really going on is that Esther, who has taken hours painstakingly attaching synthetic braided extensions to Lillian's hair, is singeing the fuzzy ends and pinching them closed to hold the braid.

"Esther," I say, "how did you learn to do this?"

"I don't know. You just watch and try it on your friends. I haven't always succeeded. I've gotten better at it over the years."

"You don't do your own hair, do you?"

"No, my sister Maureen does it."

The next day, as I wait for a car to pick me up and take me to town, Lillian rides by, being chauffeured on a bicycle. I point to my head and yell, "Lillian, looking good!" She gives me the thumbs-up sign and her beautiful smile at full voltage.

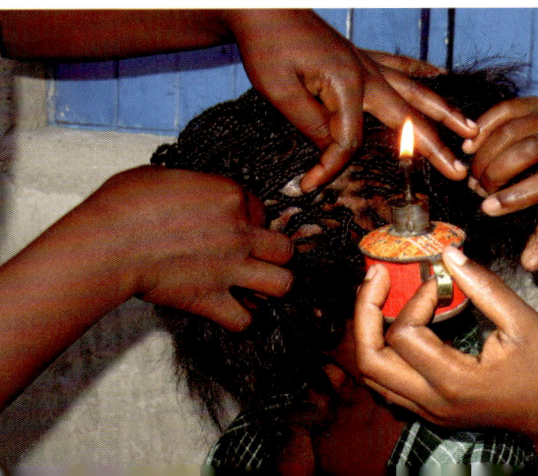

26 NOVEMBER 2011

The Bridge

There are beautiful days here and then there are astonishingly, astoundingly, unbelievably gorgeous days here. It is one of the latter as I walk up the road behind my office, talking with Edward. But the glory of the weather — billowing popcorn clouds, the massage of the warm breeze — and the grandeur of the mountains before us make his story all the more incongruent. It is a phenomenon one runs into in this place too frequently: great natural beauty that has been the setting for terrible brutality.

"At 3:00 p.m. we were told to leave," Edward says. "We all ran out from the school, went to the village. Our parents came and found us. We stayed at the Catholic Church. At night the rebels attacked. I lost two of my brothers. They kidnapped three, one came back. Two are still missing. The house we were sleeping in was totally destroyed by bullets. I saw a man open the door; he was shot dead by bullets."

"You saw that?"

"I saw that."

Edward, who lives across the courtyard from me, works for the same co-op that I do. He is in his mid-20s now, but he's telling me about what happened at the small hamlet we're walking to when he was a boy of 9. The village he refers to is the one where we live and work. The school is a 30-minute walk up the hill from my office. The rebels were the vicious Ugandan group known as the Allied Democratic Forces, based in the Democratic Republic of Congo (formerly Zaire). In 1996, the ADF swept over the Rwenzori Mountains from the DRC like a sad black wind and destroyed the school, burned it to the ground. To the degree that the ADF expresses any goals beyond thuggery, it seems to have some vague religious ideology and aspires to overthrow the government of Uganda.

Edward continues, "The ADF fired rockets up here. They would come at night and slaughter people like goats. It was very difficult for us to go back to school after being attacked. They attacked during the third term, end of the school year, so the whole next year, 1997, was wasted. There were no resources or scholastic materials. Only UNICEF came in to assist us. When they attacked, it was a new school, three years old. Two buildings with six classrooms were burned down, they also burned the school library; the offices and furniture were destroyed. They blew up the bridge with a land mine. We were scared, always suspicious — waiting for the rebels to attack us again. We were hungry; to get a meal was once in 24 hours."

The power of Edward's account is amplified by the casual, offhand way in which he tells it. He could just as well be recalling the first soccer game he attended. But when you are a child of 9, what's normal? What reference points do you have? Strange men invade your homeland, steal children, murder adults, burn your school, fire rockets at your village. Who knows? Maybe that's just what happens on any day anywhere. Besides, from his perspective, Edward's childhood was not unusual; everyone he grew up with had the same experience.

The Ugandan army finally drove out the ADF, and since 2002 this has been a peaceful area, though the repercussions of that invasion are felt to this day; a friend of mine here leads a monthly support group for women who were abducted by the ADF. (Coincidentally, this article appeared in the Kampala newspaper the day after I wrote most of this post.) This is now a highly productive coffee-growing region and the success of the coffee farming is raising the incomes of the farmers. Progress is gradual, but things are moving in a positive direction.

After things got more or less back to normal, "They began to reconstruct the bridge," Edward tells me, "but there were leftover land mines and people feared the area." Nonetheless, the bridge did get rebuilt. In fact, it's been rebuilt many times. It is crucial: Homes are on one side of the river, the school is on the other. About 500 children use the bridge twice a day going to and from school to cross a seriously powerful river. As you can see in the photograph at the top of this post, it is a graceful, picturesque span. Unfortunately, it's also dangerous. In the rainy season, the swollen, rushing waters wash away the bridge entirely. Then it's put back. It's destroyed again the next rainy season, and replaced. And so on.

"Children have been dropping in the river," Edward says. "In 2002 a 7-year-old girl fell and drowned."

Edward wants to see the bridge rebuilt as a permanent span, using concrete and steel. It should have railings and a solid deck of thick planks — a real bridge.

"How?" I ask.

"I don't know," Edward says. "Somehow."

10 OCTOBER 2011

To the Land of Endless Wanting

Now comes the journey from the Land of Endless Needing to the Land of Endless Wanting. In a few days I return to the USA after 27 months in Africa. The anticipation of this flight from one strange planet to another has generated all manner of anxiety and a jumble of bittersweet emotions. It has kept me preoccupied more than ever with thinking about the extreme differences between the two places.

Both are easily idealized and deeply flawed. Both possess terrifically positive qualities and unquestionably negative ones; neither is immune from evil, either as victims or practitioners. Africa and America are inextricably connected to and dependent on one another through centuries of history — both tragic and transcendent. If America is the light of the world — and at its best it is — then Africa is the energy source, the fuel and provenance for large pieces of America's greatness, goodness and complexity.

In Africa needs are abundant and frequently unfulfilled, but much of the culture is communal by nature, so giving and sharing are integral parts of the social structure. In America, saturated, as it is, by an advertising-driven, acquisitive culture, obsessive about personal independence, one of the most pervasive feelings is wanting — wanting, but never quite getting that want satisfied. The function of advertising is to generate want, constant want, and due to the ubiquity, intensity and sophistication of advertising in the U.S. it is enormously successful.

I think that must be one reason most Africans I've met, young and old, seem to be happier people than most Americans. Their happiness is largely derived from what they already have, which is a rich fabric of relationships and a carpe diem approach to everyday life. Americans, on the other hand, are, everywhere they go, confronted with a nonstop montage of images and sounds (J.G. Ballard called it "the media landscape") designed to make them want what they don't have. Not surprisingly, they want a lot. It is endless.

Richard Dowden wrote, "Africa never loses hope." I'd add that Africa also never lacks for enthusiasm, for heart and (need it be said?) soul — deep, dark, poignant, rich, hard, sweet as honey. Africa is a magnificently seductive place: gorgeous, dramatic, dangerous, heartbreaking and sexy. Who can resist? It gets on you, it gets in you, and then you can't do without it. Africa is a lover you must have now, over and over, all day and all night.

I return to the U.S. in a state of spiritual drunkenness, inebriated by the rush of images and feelings flashing past of the last two years.

In the midst of this wrenching, hyper review — like a film run at twice speed — it's impossible to grasp it all. I'm curious about seeing the U.S. again; eager to see the people I've missed, but, frankly, also very anxious to return here.

Now that departure is imminent, I'm just barely beginning to comprehend what a profoundly singular time this has been. Yet I also observe myself withdrawing, distancing, seeking more solitude than usual, to brace myself for the cold turkey-like experience of being rocketed, in a matter of hours, from one reality to a very, very different one.

I will be coming back here in a few weeks, but the first-time phenomenon of going into an utterly unexpected and foreign set of circumstances and having it work out so well on so many levels is about to end. When I return to Africa, things will be different.

Afterwards

When the time came, I didn't want to leave Uganda, and in a sense I never have. Ever since I departed I've been going back and forth, returning and staying for a month or two whenever I'm able. And even when I'm in the U.S., I'm in daily touch with various friends in Uganda. We text, we email, sometimes I put through a call because nothing is quite as pleasurable as hearing familiar voices.

The first time I returned to the U.S., after I'd been in Uganda for 27 months, as the jet approached San Francisco Airport, the jade-color bay rushing beneath us, runway appearing just in time, I braced myself for the reverse culture shock — being once again immersed in the luxury and splendor of America. But the shock never came. The place was so familiar to me, having lived in the U.S. for more than a half-century, that I simply slipped right back into it. I hadn't driven a car in more than two years, but I rented one at the airport, jumped on the freeway and was zipping in and out of lanes like Mr. Toad just minutes after my plane landed.

Seeing the most acute differences between Africa and America came later, over days, weeks even. After living in the communal culture of a remote Ugandan village, the isolation and loneliness of many Americans became vividly apparent. I also noticed that Americans have turned busyness into a fetish. We like to keep ourselves very, very busy, sometimes frantically so. And even when we are not busy we talk about how busy we are. We are in a hurry. We must go. We don't have time to do all the things we must do. We can't talk now. And we intentionally design our lives to be this way — perhaps not because we want to, but because we need to. Maybe it's a means of overcoming our feelings of isolation and loneliness — or a way of reinforcing them. It's certainly an effective method for keeping others at a distance.

Africa always has time, which is surely one of its most charming features. Shortly after I began living in Kyarumba, I was walking down the road in the village and a woman was walking toward me carrying a massive load of firewood on her back. Tucked above the firewood and behind her head was her baby. I pointed and smiled as if to say, "That's a pretty good balancing act." (The first thing babies learn in Africa is how to hang on.) And then I said, "Wasibere" (Good afternoon). "Yiri wahi?" (How are you?) She laughed at the fact that I knew some Lhukonzo, said, "Ni buholho" (I'm fine), then walked over and shook my hand, held it for a long moment, looked into my eyes, then laughed and continued down the road.

Africans are extraordinarily busy people, but they always have time — because they take it: like the woman carrying the firewood and her baby. She likely had several more kids at home and a full day (and night) of work ahead of her, but she stopped, gave me some of her time. That scenario would be replayed hundreds of times during the two-and-a-half years I lived there.

But every place has its deficiencies and its superfluities. Africa has the things that money can't buy and wants the things that money can buy; America has the things money can buy and wants the things that money can't buy. Neither place knows much about the other. Most Americans and Africans tend to believe the often shrill reportage of mass media, which is frequently wrong, distorted or cherry-picked, either consciously or unconsciously, to give a skewed view that is more cliché than truth. As Aldous Huxley quipped, "To travel is to discover that everyone is wrong about other countries." The more time I spent in Uganda the truer Huxley's remark became. I'm guessing that Africans who visit America find it just as true.

Perhaps the most perplexing thing about being back in the U.S. is the degree to which people don't seem to want to know more about Africa, to see it in a way that departs from their assumptions and the received wisdom they've absorbed over the years. Why? It's a mystery, a conundrum that Zambian economist Dambisa Moyo addressed specifically in a February 2013 CNN interview:

> "This is a great continent. I went to primary school on this continent, secondary school, university, I've worked on this continent and I think that it's a great disservice that, for whatever reason, people have usurped an imagery of Africa that is absolutely incorrect.

> "They focus on war, disease, corruption and poverty. That is not all about Africa and I think it's really essential if we're going to turn the corner, we need to take that responsibility, as governments, as citizens, not just Africans, global citizens to say, 'that's actually not true.'

> "There are more poor people in India than there are in Africa; more poor people in China than there are in Africa, but somehow there's a stigma for decades that's been associated with the African continent that is completely unjustified — and it's that I find objectionable."

Anyone who spends time in Africa and falls in love with it, as I have, will understand Moyo's frustration with the rest of the world's insistence on seeing the place entirely in terms of war, disease, corruption and poverty, while refusing to acknowledge the many hopeful, productive, positive things that take place there every day. Indeed, when you live in Africa, you find – not surprisingly – that in the most important ways it's much like anywhere else. What's going on most of the time in most places is that people are getting their kids off to school, cleaning their house, fixing a car, doing laundry, working in their shop or their garden, visiting friends, having a beer at a corner cafe and so on. The fabric of life is being woven daily, in much the same way, most everywhere in the world, and Africa is no exception.

Another thing the rest of the world misses out on by dismissing Africa as nothing more than an ongoing catastrophe is the fun. I've never been anywhere that fun was as integral a part of everyday life as it is in Africa. I've never laughed as hard, or as frequently, as I've laughed in Africa. And I've never danced so badly while enjoying it so much as in Africa.

Now – in my mind and heart, at least – I live in two places. With luck, I'll continue to go back and forth, splitting my time between these very different lands, resigned to the fact that the two can't really be reconciled. But then I suppose there is no reason or need to do so.

Acknowledgments

My deepest gratitude goes to the people of Kyarumba, Uganda, who took me into their
Rwenzori Mountains community and into their lives for two-and-a-half years.

I'm forever grateful to Nattabi Ruth Lugose Basoma whose enthusiasm and love for her country and
its culture, sense of adventure and fun, curiosity, intelligence and energy enriched my experience of
Uganda, and continues to every time I visit that beautiful place.

I also appreciate the help given me early on by Laurie Chu, Michael Monteleone and Pam Ingalls.

Ruth Henrich did the expert copy-editing, though any errors that may remain are entirely my own.

Tracy Cox did an outstanding job of designing the book, bringing his skill, taste,
patience and good ideas to every page as well as the cover.

This book would not exist were it not for the kindness of friends who contributed funds
to its production when it was still in the planning stage. Their names are listed below.

Contributors

Robert Stadd
Rachel Hobreigh
Fabrice & Phyllis Florin
Wendy Slick
Dana & Kira Hopper
Brian Gauvin
Patricia N. Robinson
Karen McMillan
Chris Colin

Amy Standen
Ruth Henrich
Judith Calson
Don Campau
Mark David Compton
Diane Demee-Benoit
Dan Benoit
Michal Keeley
Tom Colin

Jan Cook
David McMillan
Robert & Joan Benedetti
Kim Spencer
David Talbot
Camille Peri
Margaret Talbot
Susan Hall
Steve McKinney

Douglas Mackay
Kristina Branch
Richard Jefferies
Dennis Hoffman
Thomas & Kathleen Holliday
Whitman McGowan
Margery Snyder
David & Melissa Robinett
Susie Schlesinger

Donovan Pendell
Kevin & Jennifer Sweeney
Carol Mastick
Matthew Slavik
Sheryl Speck
Hayley White
David Jansen
Marianne Martin
Nancy Keith

"Like all great travelers, I have seen more than I remember, and remember more than I have seen."
—Benjamin Disraeli